IRISH AMERICAN HERO: MICHAEL PATRICK O'SHEA

IRISH AMERICAN HERO: MICHAEL PATRICK O'SHEA

By

Dan'l T. Sheehan

1st Books rev. 6/05/00

ABOUT THE BOOK

<u>Irish American Hero: Michael Patrick O'Shea</u>

He was born an American, but he was raised to support their cause.They wanted him to be a hero; an Irish rebel. They intended to throw him as a human sacrifice on the bloody altar of Irish freedom.There was no one who could stop him... not his friends, not the Church, not family, not the FBI, not the British Army... and not even the love a beautiful girl.

<u>DEDICATION</u>

To my wife, Pam. It was her patience, skill, and love that made this novel possible.

For Heidi McAllister and victims of violence everywhere.

Old days. The wild geese are flying
Head to the storm as they faced it before;
For where there are Irish there's memory undying
And when we forget, it is Ireland no more."
-Unknown

Ludwig Van Beethoven composed his Symphony No. 3 in 1803. He had dedicated it to Napoleon Bonaparte; a man he believed was a great hero of the democratic cause. When Napoleon had himself declared Emperor of France, Beethoven tore the dedication page up in anger. The Symphony today is called the "Eroica" in honor of its heroic spirit.

PART I

<u>Seanathair</u>

The room was dark and had a musty smell to it. The old man lay on the bed looking like a wax carving. Deep lines cut into his face. His body tensed and shook as he coughed and hacked into convulsions.

Michael's father pushed him into the room. His great-grandfather's eyes sparkled with recognition. A toothless smile welcomed them. Behind Michael's father came his grandfather, a look of deep concern on his face.

Grandfather was old but great-grandfather was even older. The biggest number Michael knew was one-hundred and great grandfather was nearly that many years old.

"You feeling any better, Grandfather?" asked Michael's father.

"Why sure, I feel like getting' up and runnin' round the block. Of course I'm not feeling any better, I'm dying!"

"Dying? Ah, Da, you'll live another 97 years."

"Bullshit" He said and coughed. Michael could hear his whistling breath. "You have all the O'Shea men under one roof and you waste my last hours with bullshit. " The old man began hacking worse than before, his entire frail body shaking with each cough.

"What do you want to talk about?" asked the grandfather.

"The family! Do you know what we are? Eh? Tell me!"

"I don't know what you mean, grandfather."

The form on the bed began to relax now, lying back and looking up at the ceiling with watery unblinking eyes.

"Wild geese! Did you know that Michaeleen?" Michael looked back at his great-grandfather on the bed. He didn't know how to reply to the question but no one took notice of the moment of silence. "We are the last of the Wild Geese!" The oldest living O'Shea spoke less to them now as he did to the air. A lifelong politician, rebel and Irish republican, he addressed an audience of memories.

"Noble birds may fly from forces they can't fight but they always return. Like the geese eh? Like the geese we are noble birds. My oldest brother died in the Fenian uprising here in America. He died for Ireland... a place he had never even seen. The Fenians were fools. Thinking' they were going to whip the English in America. They attacked Canada! Wanted to swap Canada for Ireland's freedom. You'll never hear about it in an American history book. America wants to bury us in green beer and paper shamrocks.

His voice became rasping.

"They drove back an army of Brits and then the U.S. army stepped in. My brother drowned. Driven back, they were pushed into the Niagara river...swept over the falls. I was just a little boy. Mother taught me to never forget. It was for Ireland. Part of every dollar earned went to the rebels. When I was a boy there was no Republic of Ireland and now we got two of them.

He tried to laugh but broke into coughing.

"We can't give up. Can't. We fought too long to stop now... Every generation, every Irish son. Every O'Shea... As long as they hold an inch of our homeland...

Is Eireannach me

"C'mon, O'Shea ya chicken! Fight!"

Michael Patrick O'Shea looked up from the ground, his eyes stinging with tears. The blond-haired boy who stood above him fists clenched and poised to strike, had already landed two blows for every one of his own. Michael's heart was pounding, his stomach and face ached from the shower of blows he had received. He started to push himself up on his knees and a series of kicks and punches forced him down again. He didn't want them to see him cry and tried to hold back the tears, but instead the weeping came out choked with a coughing sound.

"Look, he's crying!" one of them yelled.

"His nose is running." Another said and a machine gun-like blast of high pitched laughter rained over him.

"I think he likes it!"

"Hey! You like the taste of snot?"

"That's cause it's green snot!"

"Yeah, snotgreen! Is that Irish green O'Shea?

The laughter came in an endless downpour. He tried to get up and was beaten down once more. The blond-haired boy grabbed him by the collar and half pulled him from the ground. Face to face, Michael could smell the boy's baloney sandwich breath.

"You gunna wear that button anymore?"

Michael O'Shea didn't reply. He didn't have time to. The blond boy tore the button from his jacket. The brass pin that held it in place fell ringing on the street. The button itself, stepped on and kicked into the gutter.

"You gunna get up and fight or lay there eatin boogers?"

Michael didn't move. He could hear his heart ticking in his ears. He was angry and frightened at the same time. His stomach felt knotted. He wanted to get up but he was unsure what he would do. They kept laughing. He closed his eyes. The mocking voices seemed farther away. He held his breath and waited for silence. It came. They were gone.

4

Mike eased himself to his feet, knees shaking and choking back tears, staggered toward the muck-filled street gutter. He picked up the plastic coated button, wiped the mud off with trembling fingers; John F. Kennedy's face and the word "Elect" came to the surface, blurred and scratched.

He came home, his clothes torn and face bruised. His mother confronted him. Questions and demands poured out; had he been fighting, who did this, look at your jacket. She would never wait for a reply.

"I was looking' for crayfish in the gully and I fell down the bank."

"What!" Her voice became shrill, "You mean to tell me you did this to yourself falling in that gully?"

"Yes."

"Well, listen here young man. If you've been fighting and you're not telling me the truth...."

"Ease up on the boy!" shouted his father, slamming his racing form down on the kitchen table. "If he had a fight and lost, it's his right to handle it himself."

"Oh! I suppose we should let him come home and tell lies about how his new good school jacket was ripped. Keep right on letting him have his way. You're the one that's spoiling him!"

"Katherine, don't go giving me that. If anyone is spoiling him it's you. You'll buy him anything he wants. I'll bet he has five other jackets hanging in that closet."

"Now don't change the subject, Patrick."

"Change the subject?"

"Yes, change the subject."

"Now look," returned his father with a smile, "you're the one who started talking about the kid being spoiled!"

"That is not what we were talking about!"

"It isn't?"

"No. It isn't".

"Well then, what the hell were we talking about?"

"Oh, I don't believe it! Mikey, go get washed up for dinner."

He eased between his parent and made his way to the bathroom. The rubber plug fit funny into the drain and made the sink fill slowly. He started to wash his hands, playing with the soap and making it "jump" from his hands by squeezing it from the bottom.

Michael looked into the mirror and saw the scratches and blue-black bump on his cheek. He had the marks of a fight loser. His parents were still arguing in the kitchen, but he couldn't hear the words if he kept the water running fast. Water always seemed very peaceful, even when it raced out of the tap.

There was a lot of black stuff under his fingernails. Whenever he went outside the house it always seemed like he got some of that black stuff under his nails. It took a long time to wash it out, but if any of it was left when he came to the table he'd be made to wash again.

"Michael!" his father yelled from the kitchen, "Are you going to be in there all day? Come on the food is getting cold!" He turned off the faucet, quickly wiped his hands on the towel and hurried out to the table. Michael bowed his head and crossed himself

"Bless us O Lord for these thy
gifts which we are about to receive
From thy bounty, through Christ,
    Our Lord, Amen."

At the word "Amen" his father stabbed a fork into the bowl of steaming potatoes and set one large spud on his plate. He then mashed it down with his fork and proceeded to drown it in blobs of yellow butter.

"Dad, how come you like potatoes so much?"

"All Irish love potatoes."

"Teddy Anatolli isn't Irish, he's Italian, and he likes potatoes."

"Well, now didn't we have spaghetti just last Thursday? And you like spaghetti, don't you?"

"Sure, I do, Dad. But I don't like potatoes."

"Well, you'll eat these potatoes and you'll like them after your mother worked so hard to cook them."

"Dad, does liking spaghetti make me Italian?"

His father's face broke open with a smile. "No, being Irish is something you're born with. You can change the country you live in but not the blood in your veins."

Michael slid his fork under his potatoes and took a grim swallow.

"Dad, Kennedy will win, won't he?"

"Why sure he will. Son, it'll be a cold day in Hell before a man like Nixon could be President."

Michael smiled, the potatoes tested better.

Coirneal

Michael's collection of toy soldiers stood in a line. His hand held the one lone hero of "Z" company. One brave survivor of the battle of Mikey's bedroom. The bent tip of the plastic soldier's machine gun pointed at the would-be victors and suddenly a spray of spit roared out as Michael made his deadly machine gun noise and scattered the entire line of bad guys apart with his hands. The lone hero toy had killed the entire invading force and saved his country. Michael gave a cheer just as his cousin David came in. David was a little older than Michael and he was embarrassed to be seen playing with toy solders.

"Wow Mike! Where'd you get that extra cheek bone?" David was smiling and Michael felt some extra color come into his cheeks. "Got in a fight?"

"Yeah..."

"Come here. Let me show you something."

Michael tried to turn away but David stepped around to face him. "Did they get you on the ground?"

"Yeah.." Michael was feeling more uncomfortable and wanted to escape. David wrapped an arm around his cousin and held his attention.

"Mikey, you don't have any brothers or sisters so you never really learned to fight. Come on. Hold your hand up like this. No, like this only higher. When someone swings , you can block the punch like this. When you get a clear shot to hit back try to hit them where it will really hurt. Hit them in the neck, just below the chin, in the belly just below the ribs and if it looks like you're losing..."

"What?"

David smiled, "Kick'em in the balls!"

Mike burst out laughing and David joined him. "If you're outnumbered, use a stick or a weapon and make sure you hurt the biggest and strongest bully first. Most bullies are cowards and they run when their leader is down."

Michael saw the blond boy again in his mind.

"David, suppose they don't run?" David heard the worry in Michael's voice. "Then you give him a fight of a lifetime. If he knocks you down you get up and go at him again... and if he knocks you down again, you get up again. You get up and keep fighting as long as it takes to win."

David turned Michael to face him, so that he could look directly into his eyes. "Michael, the Irish don't quit! We fight until we win or until we're dead."

De Domhnaigh

"Introibe ad Altare Dei."

"Domine non sum dignus."

The Mass had ended. Old Father Kilclooney placed his black hat on his balding head. The people knelt and made the sign of the cross. The organ music gently filled the air. The people began to file out.

Michael O'Shea lifted the long candle snuffer high over the altar, covering the flame of each candle. He had managed to serve the entire mass without Father Kilclooney seeing that he had worn his sneakers under his cassock.

Once during the mass, when he handed him the wine, he was sure the old priest had looked right at his feet. Michael had stared up into those steel-blue eyes, expecting to see a look of anger. The expression didn't change. The placid face the Father Kilclooney always wore during mass didn't change a line.

The last of the crowd were disappearing through the arched doors, and Mrs. Murphy had finished her last chorus of "All Glory, Laud and Honor". A few old ladies finished their rosary beads. The organ trained a last breath to silence and the church became dead.

The last candle extinguished, Michael knelt before the altar and went to the rear of the church.

Father Cassidy, the young assistant priest entered the rear chambers just as Michael was covering his cassock with a dry-cleaner bag. The angular priest always reminded Michael of an oversized rat. Cassidy's face had the long pointed look of a rat and the dark hornrim glasses he wore gave his eyes a rat-like glare. Father Cassidy tended to give those hellfire sermons that Catholics didn't hear very often these days. Michael believe that the young priest actually enjoyed seeing the hair on the back of his neck stand up when he preached.

"Michael!" came Cassidy's sulfurous voice. It made even Michael's name sound like some sinful act. "Did you serve Mass wearing those sneakers?:

10

"I...ah..." A lie had begun to form on his lips, but he caught himself. "Yes, Father."

"Is that how you show your respect for God?"

"No, Father."

"How long have you been an altar boy?"

"Since last year, Father."

"A year! A year you've been an altar boy, and you still don't know enough to bring your shoes!"

Michael began to lower his head, looking down over the top of his sneakers. He heard a footstep and looked past Father Cassidy and into the calm face of Father Kilclooney.

"Father Cassidy, I'll handle this. Would you please leave us alone." Cassidy's mouth opened, almost saying the words of protest he was thinking. He grunted and quickly left the chamber. Father Kilclooney sat down heavily as though he had just finished climbing a mountain. He peeled his hat from his head and stared at Michael.

"You're the O'Shea boy, are you not?" spoke the old priest slowly. Michael replied with a nod.

"Got any brothers or sisters?"

"No, Father."

"I'll bet people tell you you're spoiled, don't they?" Michael looked down at his sinful feet again. "Yes, Father." Well, I never came by an only child who wasn't spoiled rotten. Yelling nonsense outside and inside the church. Undisciplined! They never seem to grow up either. Martin Luther was an only child, I think. Anyway, there ought to be some kind of a rule against people having only a single child. It is almost unchristian! You and that little Italian boy are the worse of the lot of them. He's an only child too, isn't he?"

"Yes, Father."

"Well, you think I didn't see you two after Mass last Sunday, splashing each other with the Holy water? I had to clean up the mess you left. You're ashamed of yourself, aren't you Michael?"

"Yes, Father."

"That's why I want you to try to be a little smarter and remember to bring your shoes. Okay?"

"Yes, Father."

11

"Of course, the Irish always spoil their sons. Father's a Kerryman, I'll bet."

"No, Father."

"O'Shea is an old Kerry name. What then? Your Grandfather?"

"No, Father. My family has been in America since before my great, great, great grandfather."

"Well then, how can you say you're Irish?"

"Because we are."

"Then you're Hiberniores hibenis ipsos, eh?"

"What?"

Father Kilclooney smiled broadly, "Hiberniores hibenis ipsos. It's Latin. Means more Irish than Irish. I figure it applied to those families who haven't forgotten where they came from. Families who have kept their roots. The families who stay Irish even when it isn't St. Patrick's Day. Ah, no doubt you've been raised Irish from birth, am I right? Cad e mar ta tu?"

"Oh, Go maith, go raibh maith agat, Father."

"And your father's made you study the Irish, too?"

"I'm not very good at it, Father."

"Ha! Well, course you wouldn't know if you was or you wasn't. I've never met your father, but I've heard his name a few times around the Hibernian Hall. I'll have to have a talk with him sometime... Ah, anyway you had better be getting home now."

Michael pulled on his jacket quickly. He knew his parents would be waiting. He headed for the exit.

"And Michael!" shouted Father Kilclooney after him, "If people are teasing you about being an only child, remind them of this." He pointed to the crucifix on the wall, "Christ was an only child, too."

O'cinn'eide

"Children," came the Principal's voice over the intercom, "We have some sad news. The President is dead."

Michael O'Shea looked down in the grain of his desk. He had heard the news, heard it from the Principal himself, but he didn't believe it. He didn't want to believe. A sick feeling crawled into his stomach. He wanted to go home.

The school was closed. The children loaded on the buses. Each bus became alive with excitement. The bus door creaked closed. The shouting and laughter blurred into a massive roar of noise. Only a few wild shouts broke through into Michael's consciousness.

Kennedy had been a hero to his family. He was the only Irish Catholic to ever be elected President. He was living proof that the Irish had "made it" in America. Now he was murdered.

Michael's grandfather had claimed that the O'Sheas were distantly related to the Kennedy family by ancient clan ties with the Dalcassians. It was funny. Kennedy was a hero in World War II but to Michael he didn't have a hero's name.

"Bet it was Nixon who killed him?" someone shouted.

Can a name make an ordinary person a hero? O'Shea seemed like a good name for a hero... though no hero he could think of had ever carried the name. His family history talked about many people named O'Shea who were heroes. His grandfather spent hours telling stories of how O'Sheas had fought in revolt after revolt against British rule in Ireland. But these people were heroes only to his own family, no one else.

"Texas, Texas people did it. They killed him to start the Civil War again!" Broke in another wild yell.

Sarsfield, Tone, Pearse and Connolly were all Irish heroes. They gave up their lives for their cause even when they know there was no hope of victory. Robert Emmet was a martyr for Ireland. He had tried to rebel against English rule and failed. The British had him hanged. They cut off his head and displayed it.

They cried out to the crowds who saw his execution, "This is the head of Robert Emmet, a traitor." His blood had run down the street gutters and the old women dipped their handkerchiefs in it. The handkerchiefs were saved over generations and prized as almost a religious symbol. Even today you could still find Robert Emmet's portrait in Irish homes, hanging beside the crucifix. Now there would be portraits of Kennedy there as well.

O'Shea. O'Shea! The name had the sound of clashing steel in it. If you said the name just right you could almost see two warrior chieftains crossing swords. It was a hero's name. It seemed that anyone with a name like that should be a hero.

"I hope they kill the guy that did it!" came another shout.
When Michael played now he would be Ireland's ancient hero Cuchulain and his older cousin David would be the blond-haired warrior Feriad. They would meet in the shallow waters of the brook that flowed by Michael's house. There they would battle with wooden swords and shields as the heroes of ancient Eire had done. War cries in Gaelic would be shouted.

Michael would become a hero, an Irish hero...like Cuculain, like Emmet, like Kennedy!

The voice and noise on the bus began to overpower his thoughts, mixing in with them.

"I wish I could kill the guy that did it!"

"Think we'll get tomorrow off?"

"Does this make Nixon the President now?"

"They said we might get a week or more off. Maybe it's 'cause they got to wait and find the guy that shot him."

"Hope they catch him here in South Boston, and we get to kill him."

How many days off are we gunna get do you think?"

"Will they hang the guy or shoot him?"

"Bet it's a lie! I bet he's not dead!"

"Whoever did it I'd kill him. I'd...

"The Russians did it! No, Cuba!"

"If there's a war we'll...let's see if we can catch him. "

" My Dad's got a gun."

"He's not dead. How many days? We can play stick ball. They must know who did...

15

"Think we'll have school...Texas? They'll kill.

Russian! War! Play! Kill!

Lie! Kill! Shot! Kill! Play! Kill.

The bus door creaked open. Michael stepped off. The large orange machine rumbling behind him gave a shudder and moved on. He walked up the gravel driveway and entered the house.

Nothing seemed to move for days. Hardly a word was spoken as the days of mourning passed. A week went by. It was as if a member of the family had died. There was only quiet. The shades were drawn, the house kept dark. A silence as Michael had never known hung over his home.

Michael looked into the living room. His father was bent over, his head in his hands, trembling, sobbing, before the flickering light of the television. Uniformed soldiers carried the casket from the horse-drawn cart.

He looked again at his father. Why? Fathers don't cry.

Patrick O'Shea looked up, saw his son, and drew him to his side.

16

Ireland

A Report by Michael Patrick O'Shea
Miss Switzer's Social Studies Class
May 22, 1966   Bishop Martin Junior High

"My report is on Ireland." said Michael stiffly as he stood in the front of the class.

"Ireland is an island country west of Great Britain in the North Atlantic. Ireland is about the size of New York State. It is a divided country. Twenty-six counties make up the Republic of Ireland and six northern counties make up Northern Ireland which is part of Great Britain. People have lived in Ireland for a very long time...."

The first humans reached Ireland around 6000 B.C. They were known in Irish mythology as the Firbolg. A peaceful farming people, they built huge stone tombs like New Grange hundreds of years before the rise of the first Egyptian pyramid.

The Celtic people invaded Ireland around 350 B.C. They were warlike and the peaceful Firbolg disappeared. The Celts had a system of law, a writing system and a government of clans and chieftains.

Christianity was brought to Ireland around 400 AD When the Roman Empire fell, Europe became overrun by pagan invaders. Ireland was a home for large numbers of Christians and scholars. While most of Europe fell into the true "dark age", Ireland was the center of peace and learning. A number of Irish saints rekindled Christianity in England, Scotland, France and even as far away as northern Italy. Irish monks, in their missionary zeal, traveled across the Atlantic and are said to have reached America 1000 years before Columbus.

The wealth of the Irish churches drew the interest of the Vikings around the year 800. For the next 200 years, there was constant warfare. King Brian Boru finally united Ireland and drove out the Vikings in 1014.

Adrian IV, the one and only English Pope, gave Ireland to English King Henry II but the English invaders never got much beyond the city of Dublin. Ireland, for the most part, continued as it always had.

The tiny area of Ireland ruled by the English was called "the Pale" and the rest of Ireland, "beyond the Pale" was independent.

When the fat English King Henry VIII, wished to divorce his wife; broke with the Catholic Church and declared himself head of the Church of England and Ireland, the Irish resisted. They resisted more in Northern Ireland under the clan leadership of the O'Donnells and O'Neils.

The rebels finally lost at the Battle of Kinsale in 1602 and rather than simply surrender to English rule they fled to mainland Europe. Their followers became famous mercenary soldiers known as the "Wild Geese".

This opened the way for the beginning of the "plantation of Ireland". The lands of the Irish nobles were to be given to poor, but loyal people from Scotland and England. Thousands of Scottish lowlanders who swore a loyalty oath were given Irish lands. Ironically, many of those Scots were descended from Irish settlers who had moved to Scotland centuries ago.

In 1641, a religious maniac named Oliver Cromwell, overthrew the English king and installed a Puritan government. The Irish rebelled and Cromwell invaded Ireland, massacred the population , took away all land from the native Irish and all their political rights. Without a doubt, Oliver Cromwell was Ireland's first real conqueror.

After Cromwell's death, the British monarchy was restored and James II became King. Since James II was a Catholic, he abolished many of the anti-Catholic laws. James II was overthrown in 1688 by Protestant extremists. King James went to the one territory of his kingdom where the vast majority of people were Catholics. He went to Ireland , and then he raised an army.

The English Protestants had placed William of Orange on the throne and he then invaded Ireland. James II was defeated in 1690 at the Battle of the Boyne.

William of Orange took all remaining land from the Irish. Catholics could not purchase or inherit land. They could not have weapons or join the army. The practice of the Catholic faith was forbidden and priests would be executed if they were caught. Large numbers of Irish Catholics were sold as slaves in the Caribbean or driven to the barren rocky western part of Ireland.

The American, and later French revolutions inspired the Irish and, ironically, led by Protestants, Ireland rebelled in 1798 under a man named Wolfe Tone. In 1804, there was another failed rebellion under Robert Emmet.

The native Irish were reduced to being farm workers who "rented" the land. Rents were paid in crops. The Irish were allowed to keep potatoes for their food supply. Living in such extreme poverty, the worst in all of Europe, the Irish depended on the potatoes for almost their entire diet.

In 1845 through 1847, a plant disease destroyed the potato crops. Ireland's population in 1845 was estimated at 8 million people. When the potato famine ended, Ireland's population was reduced to less than half. With a strong belief in the Protestant "work ethic" and laissez-faire economics, the British did virtually nothing while the Irish starved.

Ireland lost many of its people due to emigration. The Irish who reached America did not forget their roots and formed the Fenians. In the 1860's, they received battle training fighting in the American Civil War. The Fenians hired the inventor John Holland to build a secret weapon, a submarine named the Fenian Ram to destroy the British Navy. The Fenians built up an army and stockpiled weapons. Many American politicians secretly supported the Fenians in hope of starting a war with Britain that would give them an excuse to seize Canada. The Irish invaded and captured Fort Eire in Canada, but President Grant interfered and the Fenians had to give up. The Fenian Ram was taken by the U.S. Navy and Fenian rebels in Ireland were hanged.

In 1916, while Britain was locked in mortal combat with Germany in World War I, the Irish rebelled again and failed again. The leaders were executed. The executions created great sympathy for the rebels. In 1919, Ireland again declared itself an independent nation. The Irish Republican Army launched a guerrilla war. The British responded by sending a special military police force called the Black and Tans to Ireland.

The fighting continued until 1921 when Great Britain and Ireland agreed to a treaty. Ireland, or twenty-six counties of it, became a "free state" and Ulster remained under British control.

The I.R.A. refused to accept a compromise of their republic and Civil War followed in 1922 to 1923. The fighting stopped but the I.R.A. has continued to struggle for a united Ireland.

The twenty-six counties of Ireland declared themselves a totally independent republic in 1949...

"Thank you for listening to my report." Michael said and handed his paper to the teacher.

Searbh Milis

"Ready? Wrestle!?

Michael O'Shea felt the hard arms catch him down and under his arms. There was a roar from the crowd and the visiting team cheered. He'd been too slow. He was going down on the mat. He tried to twist his body to bring his opponent down and over and throw him. It didn't work. He'd second guessed Michael's plan and came down right on top of him. The Ref's face was suddenly right there waiting to pound the mat and signal a pin. Desperately Michael arched his back and lifted his body up.

"C'mon fag." Hissed the boy on top, "Give it up, you're beat!"

Michael's face burned into a bright red.

"I'm not beat!" He screamed into the boy's ear and suddenly threw his legs into the air twisting and kicking. He unexpectedly rose up and over the boy's body and came down feeling an explosion in his left arm. He was on top. Screaming in pain, Michael slammed his body against his opponent and drove him into the mat. The ref banged out the signal for a pin and Michael released the boy. He slowly stood. His left arm hung far too low and felt as if it were on fire.

"What the Hell did you do?" Shouted Coach Costello. "Jesus H. Christ! Michael! You dislocated your shoulder. What the Hell-kind-of-move was that?"

"The winning move coach." Said Michael, "I won."

"Oh, yeah! You won all right. You won being out for the rest of the season. Kid, you've got to look at what the cost of a victory might be sometimes."

Biodh deoch againn

The Hibernian Hall was filled that night. Michael wasn't really all that interested in politics but his cousin David had dragged him in and being a year older had promised to buy him a glass or two of beer in the privacy of the Irish only club.

Padraig Siochain, a representative of Sinn Fein, the political wing of the Irish Republican Army, stood on the stage. Behind him, tacked to the wall was the American Flag and the blue and white "starry plough", the flag of the official wing of the I.R.A. A large white screen was set up between the two flags and high on a stand in the center of the audience was a slide projector. There was a short benediction by Father Kilclooney and an introduction by the local president.

It had never been extraordinary for a member of the I.R.A. to speak at a Hibernian Hall but in the past they had always been old men who spoke of the conflicts as something out of history. They talked about the 1916 Rising in Dublin or the Black n'Tan war. Michael could instantly see this was going to be different. This was a young Irishman who carried a Gaelic name.

His accent was slight and he spoke slowly for his American listeners. He walked back and forth on the stage and leveled his eyes so that each man would feel he spoke directly to him.
"Gentleman, I was asked to come here for two reasons. The first was to provide you with some firsthand account of what is currently happening in Ireland and the second reason is to enlist your help. It is my belief that the first reason will provide motivation for the second quite naturally.

As most of you know, the six counties of Northern Ireland have remained under British control since the signing of the Anglo-Irish treaty in London on December 6, 1921. Just as December seventh is America's "Day of Infamy" so it is for Ireland on December sixth. The Irish Republican Army which won our Independence has never accepted the provision in that treaty which allowed for the continued oppression of our people in the North.

"We must clearly face the truth that our brothers and sisters in the north are as oppressed as the Blacks in the American south and the colored peoples of South Africa

"We have tried peaceful resolutions and non-violence. We modeled our civil rights efforts on those of Dr. Martin Luther King. We had peaceful demonstrations to ask the British to grant the Irish in Northern Ireland equal voting rights, equal rights to work. Our peaceful marches were met with stoning and shooting.

"We often hear the news media use the terms "Protestant or Catholic" to refer to the divided sides of "sectarian" violence. You must be aware the British government has cut out all foreign journalists and only the government's British News corporation is allowed to provide the world with information about what is going on there. The very name "sectarian" is only a propaganda trick to confuse the real issues. There are Protestants in the I.R.A. and good Catholics who enjoy British rule and wish to see it continue. We prefer to use the terms Nationalist or Republican to define ourselves and Loyalist to define those who wish to remain with the British.

"The Nationalists have tended to be of old Irish ancestry and the Loyalists have tended to be descended from the "plantation" setters that came to Ireland under Queen Elizabeth I, over three hundred years ago. The Queen at the same time simply gave her subjects some land in Ireland in exchange for their loyalty. Religion is just a smoke screen since many of Ireland's greatest rebel leaders were Protestants. Wolfe Tone and Robert Emmet were Protestants. One of our leaders today, John Stephenson, who changed his name to Sean MacStiofain, is a Protestant leader of the I.R.A.

"The Nationalists in Ulster simply wanted equal rights. They were peacefully protesting when they were met by the British police on the night of August 14, 1969. The British police turned their 0.30 Caliber Browning machine guns on the people of Northern Ireland."

The house lights instantly darkened and the screen suddenly came to life. Image after image of one bloody body after another appeared.   A wave of shock and revulsion poured from the screen into the crowd, Siochain continued.

"The I.R.A. had remained out of the civil rights struggle until this night.   One-hundred-fifty-five civilians were killed or wounded. The people had no one else to turn to. Who could they call for help? The police? They were the ones doing the shooting.! The British Army? Who do you suppose provided the police with the machine guns? The people turned to the Irish Republican Army. Of course, we were totally unprepared to fight. We brought in guns from over the border in Dundalk. We counterattacked with petrol bombs and then high-jacked the city buses and used them to close off the streets leading to the Nationalist ghettoes. We began building the barricades that still form the battle lines. The I.R.A. was out manned, out gunned and surprised but we still saved the Nationalists of Belfast from what surely would have been genocide. It would have been like the Nazis and the Jews in the Warsaw ghetto all over again! Since the police failed in their attempts to massacre us, the British Army has been moved in as "peacekeepers".

The slides now showed British soldiers walking the streets with machine guns, helmets and full battle dress. Armored cars, tanks and frightened women and children appeared in the next pictures. Another picture showed a cocky looking soldier with a sadistic smile stringing razor wire across a neighborhood street.

Siochain stepped directly in front of the screen and seemed to emerge out of the Belfast street of soldiers and wire. "They are an army of occupation if one every existed on this earth! The Irish people are looking to their brothers and sisters in America for help. We know you have always been there. In 1798, it was the Irish Americans who inspired and assisted Wolfe Tone and Robert Emmet. In 1867, it was the Irish Americans who paid for the arms and even the ships used in the Fenian rising. In 1916, when Patrick Pearse stood on the steps of the Dublin Post Office and read the proclamation of the republic, it was with the support of Irish Americans. It is in our "declaration of independence". Irish Americans were there with money and arms and even fought with the I.R.A..

"Today, the I.R.A. is faced with a war. It is a war that will finally unite the six counties of Ulster with the rest of Ireland. It will not be an easy task. The I.R.A. has been at peace for nearly 50 years. We are facing a modern war against a modern army. We must face the British machine guns with bolt action rifles left over from World War II. We are not asking for money to buy blankets and baby bottles. "The British government passed the Special Powers Act ending all civil and human rights. There is no freedom of speech. You can be arrested and imprisoned for any length of time for any reason. It appears that being Irish means you're guilty. We are facing an enemy every bit as evil as the Nazis. The blood flowing on the Belfast and Derry streets is every bit as red as your own. It is Irish blood and I appeal to you as fellow Irishmen for your assistance."

The final slide came up in full color. It brought a gasp of horror from the audience and tears to the eyes of some. It showed the bullet ridden body of a young mother laying dead in the street and her tiny child, wounded, missing fingers, screaming by her side.

Punt

"We're collecting." David Murphy had his eyes fixed on the fat bartender. Michael O'Shea tried to match his older cousin's look and adjusted the green, white and orange Tam O'Shanter hat to have the correct tilt. The bartender's eyes rolled in the fatty pockets of his eyelids and looked from one to the other.

"Shit!" He said with a voice that sounded almost if he was gargling fat. "We already made a donation to the I.R.A."

"Where are your donation cans, Pete?" asked David.

"Part of our little agreement was that you'd have a donation can set on every table in the bar."

The fat bartender tossed his wet towel on the bar and leaned forward.

"Look, I took them down. That Irish Republican Army shit is bad for business. People see the news and think I'm backing a bunch of terrorists."

Michael feigned a face of sympathy. "It's too bad. Here it is St. Patrick's Day and Pete O'Connell's Irish Pub makes money off its Irish name but the man won't support the Irish people. "

David patted the fat man's arm. "You're doing really well tonight, Pete. Don't you think you ought to share in the wealth a little?"

Helplessly, Pete O'Connell moved his eyes from one young man to the other. "God damn it!" He shouted and opened the cash register. He slammed a hundred dollar bill on the bar.

"Now get the fuck out!:

David palmed it slowly and pocketed the money.

"Where to next?" asked Michael.

"The 'Blarney Stone' is just down the block, but we'll have to get a pint of stout there first before we tell them we're collecting."

An ceann

Professor O'Faolain marked a sweeping chalk line on the board. Michael quickly opened his notebook. The rather chunky man at the front of the classroom moved a lock of gray hair away from his coke-bottle thick glasses and continued.

"I don't know exactly what motivates a group of young collegiate to get up at eight in the morning to study Irish Literature but I can assume from the list of names on my last list that nearly all of you are of Irish ancestry. Our focus will be on the Irish Renaissance, a period roughly between 1885 and 1940, in which the Irish defined themselves both politically and socially. It was largely the writing of O'Casey and W.B. Yeats who helped to create the nationalist agitation which finally culminated in war with England. The British by the 1870's had completely conquered the Irish. The Irish language and culture were nearly gone. Just like the American Indian, with their culture system gone, their "heroes" if you will, they turned to drink and became the butt of jokes as a race of alcoholics. It was only after Yeats and Lady Augusta Gregory, a pair of mystics exploring Irish mythology; did the Irish begin to see themselves as a people of worth again. Yeats and Gregory started by writing plays about Irish heroes like Cuchulain and Finn. Their small playhouse, the Abbey Theatre, became the source of national pride. It was the writers who created the "Irish hero". Heroes, that inspire the young men who even today join the Irish Republican Army. They fight without rest, without pay and often without hope. Shot or imprisoned by the superior British army, they became martyrs for their cause. Even those who were merely locked up as "criminals" saw themselves as Irish heroes and went on hunger strikes, willingly starving themselves to death.

W.B. Yeats saw what he had created following the great rebellion and the event was recorded in his poem "Easter 1916. The poem is haunting in the lines that show that Yeats was in fact disturbed by the "excess of Love" for the Ireland he had created. He was actually frightened by the very Irish heroes he had helped to create and repeated over and over in his poem that: "A terrible beauty is born".

<u>Currach</u>

The car roof hummed as David piloted the vehicle down the highway. The dented aluminum canoe was tied solidly to the roof rack and the back seat was filled with camping gear.

Michael stared ahead at the low rolling mountains of New York's Adirondack Park. The late fall foliage was an explosion of red, orange and green. Indian summer warmth encouraged them to roll down the windows of David's old rusted Buick Electra.

"What do you think?" asked David.

Michael looked at the scenery.

"It's beautiful" he replied.

"No. I mean my wheels! My car!"

"Well. It's okay" said Michael.

"Okay? It might not look like much but she has a 455 4-barrel V8! That is the biggest car engine Detroit ever made!"

David glanced over at his cousin, Michael, and noticed he was unimpressed.

"Let me show you something!" David's foot dropped onto the gas peddle and Michael suddenly felt his back pushed deeper into the seat.

The car roof hum turned into a roar as the old Buick zoomed past car after car.

The speedometer needle swung to 120 mph and stopped.

"What do you think now?" shouted David.

"Jesus Christ! Slow down!" Michael yelled.

"You're going to get us killed!"

David eased his foot off the gas.

"Fraid of dying?" he asked sarcastically.

"No. I'm afraid of dying because of your stupidity.

David looked over at Michael and laughed. He slowed the car to only ten miles over the speed limit They followed route 28 up passing the town of Old Forge until it jointed route 30 at Blue Mountain Lake. When they reached Long Lake, they turned off onto an old dirt road. They stopped at a state campground on the shore of Forked Lake.

Summer was over so the area was nearly deserted. David parked the car and walked right over to the lake. He bent over and took a double handful of lake water and drank it.

Michael took a breath. The air was warm but with just a touch of fall coolness. There was a scent of pine. The lake was a dark blue mirror reflecting the fall colors of the mountain above it.

David spun on his heel and headed back toward the car. "C'mon let's load the canoe!"

The canoe lifted easily off the rack and set lightly down on the water. It settled down lower in the lake as they packed a tent, sleeping bags and fishpoles into it. David set a rifle case on top and lashed everything into the canoe with clothesline.

They pushed off and paddled smoothly up the lake. A loon watched and dove under them as they went by.

"Look at the trees on the shoreline" said Michael. "They're all cut even on the bottom like someone trimmed them. What does that? Winter ice from the lake?"

"No." David replied. "The trees are trimmed up as high as the tallest deer can reach. There is no balance of nature in the Adirondacks. They don't have any wolves or predators here. They hunted them all off years ago. Now the deer overpopulate and then starve to death in the winter. That's why," he patted his rifle case, "I'm doing those deer a favor by giving them a quick easy death."

They paddled to a wide bay where the Raquette River entered the lake.

David stopped paddling and put his fishing pole together. He opened a small tin of worms, forced a soft body onto a hook and cast a line out over the smooth water. A moment later the tip of his rod was twitching and Michael smiled as a hand-sized tiger-striped perch was flopped into the canoe

They traveled up the river past a set of rapids. They fought to paddle up and then made camp near a bend in the stream.

They put up their small nylon tent and pulled the canoe on shore. David pulled his rifle out of its gun case.

"See this?" David asked. "This is a .303 British Lee Enfield. It is the favorite sniper rifle of the I.R.A. I bought this one the last time I was in Canada. It has a ten shot clip, a bolt action and..." David paused dramatically, "a pop-up peep sight!"

"Can I try it?" Michael asked.

The rifle felt heavy in his hands, but somehow it imparted an almost electric sense of power. David showed Michael how to chamber a shell and use the peep sight.

They floated tree branches and small logs out on the river as targets.

Firing at the logs, Michael felt exhilaration when a bullet struck wood, but an almost equal thrill when the bullet missed and sent up an explosive splash of water.

Michael was taking aim at a white spot on a dark floating log when David tapped his arm.

"Look over there." He whispered and pointed to a raccoon crossing a log jam on the other side of the river.

"Shoot it" hissed David.

The small gray and black animal was oblivious to them and was waddling toward the water's edge. Its ringed tail dragged behind it.

Michael leveled the iron sights of the Enfield on the raccoon's head. The sights wouldn't stay lined up. Michael suddenly realized his hands were shaking. He couldn't keep the rifle still. He fired and missed badly. A useless patch of grass blew up in the air far to the right of the little animal. The raccoon dashed off into the woods.

David smiled sympathetically.

"Buck fever." He said. "Your brain was filling your hands with doubt and your hands shook. It's always harder to kill than to shoot at a non-living target."

"How do I get over it?" asked Michael.

"You'll have to make a kill. You have to get yourself so you won't hesitate. You know the Army spends weeks training soldiers how to kill. It's not a natural thing for people to do. You have to learn it...Hey! I've got some steel-jacketed military issue bullets...You know the kind that'll go right through a bullet-proof vest. Want to see what it does to a tree?"

David opened a box of shells. He pointed out the metal covering on the bullet that made these shells so different from hunting bullets. A bullet used for deer hunting was made of lead so it flattened into a mushroom shape when it hit a deer or other animal. It stopped quickly in flesh. The metal jacketed bullets had a steel coating that gave them much greater penetration.

"Watch this." David said and chambered a round. He fired at a pine tree that was about five inches in diameter. The bullet flew clean through the tree, exploding out of the back with a thundering crack and then into a tree behind it and exploding out the back of that one as well.

David looked over at Michael with a sly smile.

"Can you imagine what a bullet like that could do to a British soldier in Northern Ireland?"

Michael nodded.

David put his hand on Michael's shoulder. "We're going to bring this stuff to Ireland someday. You and I."

Night settled and David and Michael looked up at the stars while the campfire popped and crackled. The Autumn chill made the air clear. David passed Michael a small flask of whiskey and Michael reluctantly took a swallow and tried not to hack it back up.

David stared up at the stars. "Beautiful, isn't it? America is a wonderful place. I always find it very ironic that the Irish had their land taken over and then they came here and helped take this land away from the Indians."

Michael nodded in agreement.

David took a long swallow of whiskey. "The Irish and the Indians have a lot in common. Some evil assholes come in, take their land, their religion and their language and then leave them with nothing turn to but booze. Did you ever notice there are only two ethnic groups with the reputation of being drunks; the Irish and the American Indian?"

Michael agreed. "Yes, they even conquered them the same way...Are you saying we should give America back to the Indians and Ireland back to the Irish?"

"Maybe." David replied. "If Northern Ireland belongs to the Irish, shouldn't North America belong to the American Indian?"

"Well..." Michael though a moment. "In Northern Ireland, the Nationalists make up nearly half the population and in America the Indians don't even make up ten percent."

"So, you're saying if you do a real good job of killing off the native population you don't ever owe anything to the survivors? Don't you think the blacks should own South Africa, too."

"David, are you saying that everyone should go back to where they came from?"

"No, no, Michael. People need their own countries, but they can't have the right to oppress the minorities within their borders."

"Well, if people weren't so busy oppressing each other...there'd be no need of rebels like us."

They crawled inside the tent and slipped into their sleeping bags. Michael felt the small rocks, sticks, and the uneven ground beneath his back. He could hear the river and the rapids outside and every noise in the woods. It took him hours to finally fall asleep.

Michael's eyes flicked open and he stared up into the pattern of the ripstop nylon of the tent roof. The sun was up. Michael brought his face out of his sleeping bag and felt the morning chill on his cheeks.

He nudged David. David moaned and curled into a fetal position deeper into his sleeping bag.

Michael unzipped his bag, pulled on his cold hiking boots and crawled out of the tent.

There was a low white mist hanging over the river. Michael reached back into the tent and took the Enfield rifle out. The campfire was down to a pile of warm white ashes. The grass and rocks had a light coating of frost. He shivered and put on his jacket.

Michael looked out over the river. It was covered in a low hanging white fog. The sky and mountains above were clear and blue and washed with yellow sunshine. Michael put the rifle in the canoe and then pushed the boat out into the water and hopped into it.

He paddled slowly and quietly enjoying the natural sound of the river. Michael let the boat drift silently. He came to a small grassy point that was partly bathed in sunlight. In a moment, Michael saw a deer appear there out of the mist. He slowly reached down and brought up the rifle.

Michael's eyes met the deer's and he placed the sights. The deer stared and blinked. Then the buck snorted and two long puffs of steam escaped its nostrils. Michael pulled the trigger. The rifle slammed back against his shoulder and the canoe turned. He couldn't see the deer. He set down the rifle and picked up the paddle. Michael brought the canoe to shore. He climbed out. He could see that the deer had two three- inch spike antlers and was twitching trying to stand. Michael saw himself reflected in the deer's large frightened black eyes.

"I'm sorry." Michael said.

He aimed the rifle again and fired. The shot echoed and echoed again and again.

David had a fire going and a pot of coffee by the time Michael paddled the canoe back to camp.

"Wow!" shouted David. "You bagged one down! Congratulations! Venison anyone? (Smiling, he shook Michael's hand.) How do you feel?"

Michael stared at the dead animal in the bottom of the canoe.

"I didn't like it." he replied.

"Oh, Mikey. Now how will you ever shoot a British soldier if you have second thoughts about killing a deer?"

Gae Bolga

"Congratulations!" came a mob of voices.

"Oh, I'm so happy for you, Michael." His Aunt Alana came rushing at him. He started to pull away but she had caught and embraced him with arms of fatty affection. Cousin David pulled a finger away, and the trap opened.

"Don't squash him there, Aunt Alana. Here, have a drink, Mike!" said David holding out a glass of dark liquid.

"No thanks, Dave. I don't like whiskey."

C'mon, all us Irish can drink. You want my sister and her Dago boyfriend to think they're at an Italian graduation party?"

"Well, since you put it that way."

David set the drink into Michael's hand and clicked his own glass to it.

"Slainte!" he said with a smile.

"Yeah, Slainte! returned Michael.

"Michael!" called his mother from the next room. "Kevin MacKinney's here!"

"Kevin! When did you get out?" shouted Mike as he worked his way across his relatives, clasping the large fellow's hand at the doorway.

"Three days ago. I'm out for good!"

"Ah, Kevin. You should have stayed in college. Nixon's pulling out of Viet Nam now. You could have missed the entire thing!?

"I didn't want to miss it. I had a chance to serve my country." returned Kevin. "Anyway, congratulations!"

"Thank you Kevin." smiled Michael. "Come with me sailor, I'll see your glass is filled." Mike lead Kevin across the room to a large keg of beer setting in the middle of a wash tub filled with ice. His Uncle Shane was talking loudly to a group as they guarded the beer tap. "...so we were coming back up from Florida and Tommy gets us stopped for speeding through South Carolina. The policeman stops us and checks the back of the station wagon. He shines the light in the back and comes round.

"Holy shit!" he says, "What the hell are you doing with all those guns?" And you know what Tommy says to the man? He says we're on our way on a little hunting' trip to Alaska! And the cop...he believes him!" The group of men exploded with laughter.

"Well," cried James Patrick O'Shea, "It may be my son's college graduation, and the Lord knows we're all proud of him, but this family has got itself two heroes today! As grandfather and head of this family, I'd like to make a toast to Michael and Shane!" There was a cheer and more drinks were poured. Shane's back was patted across the room. Father Kilclooney gave the blessing and they all sat down to eat.Kevin MacKinney worked his way beside Michael at the table.

"Mike," spoke up Kevin as the chicken was passed," after dinner I wonder if I could talk with you?"

"Sure, Kevin, what about?"

"Oh, not here."

"Look now, Kevin...Let's take our plates out in the backyard. We'll give old Aunt Alana our seats and she can have a better place to sit and gossip."

"Yeah, that's a good idea, Mike."

The old screen door creaked open as they pushed out into the sun. The wind was still and the early summer heat beat down on them. Michael took a drumstick between his teeth and tore off a bite.

"Mike, I know it's not my place...I think...Well.."

Michael looked up at him and swallowed hard the piece of chicken he had been chewing. "You mean my Uncle Shane and Cousin David running guns to Ireland? Its just part of a family tradition. As far back as anyone can remember, we've always sent money, arms, clothing, whatever was needed, whenever there was a rising of any kind

"Your family does all this? Don't you realize you could all go to jail?"

Kevin, the Jews send money and arms to Israel. In Miami, the Cubans are allowed to raise an entire army to free their country. The only difference between them and us is that the U.S. Government supports them and condemns us."

"Yeah, Mike, I know. I've heard that crap about Ireland since we were kids. I never thought it would lead to this kind of shit!"

"You've been out of the loop for four years in the Navy. Ireland was at peace when we were kids."

"Mike, I don't understand. My family is Irish, too. We don't support any movement. We were immigrants, too. We consider ourselves Americans."

"And that's why you don't understand! We're not immigrants. No true Irishman calls himself an immigrant. We're exiles! We were driven out! Either by famine, unemployment or war the result was the same. The British tried to exterminate us. They killed thousands of Irish men, women, and children. They sold thousands more into slavery. They created the economic system that lead to the great famine and then they took the food that the starving grew and sold it in Scotland and France! They grew fat off Irish blood, like human leeches! They made profit while a million people starved to death. They forced more than half the population out of their own country! We aren't immigrants! We're exiles!"

"Mike, all this was a long time ago..."

"It's still going on, Kevin! Pick up a newspaper!"

"But how long is your family going to keep this up?"

"Until we win. Every member of this family does what is expected of them."

"What'll be expected of you? You're an only child, the last of them. The only person left to carry on the name. What do they have in mind for you? Twenty years in prison? Maybe if you work really hard you can get yourself shot for treason. Can't you see what you're doing? Ever since we were kids every one said you O'Sheas were stuck up. Always talking about how noble you were. The last of the Wild Geese! Ireland's last great heroes. Your family has brainwashed you."

Michael suddenly turned his back on Kevin. Kevin stepped around and looked at Michael's face for a moment, searching for some reaction. Michael bit his lower lip and stared back. Kevin turned and walked away.

The party moved into the night. Drinks poured, refilled. Cheers and praises were given. Father Kilclooney ended it all with a blessing:

> "Sacred heart of Jesus, protect us
> Have mercy on us
> Mary, Queen of Ireland,
> Pray for us. Guide us."

The family began to break into its smaller units. Each unit entering a car. Headlights beamed and crisscrossed the yard moving and turning onto the road, then passing down the road until only a faint outline of light could be seen along the tree tops.

Standing on the front porch, Michael watched them disappear, one by one. He pulled the ring off the top of his beer and sipped the foam from the can. A hand touched his shoulder; he turned and saw David's face.

"Michael, I'd like to ask you to become active."

"Active?"

"You'll have to make a run."

"I don't know, Dave, I don't think..."

"C'mon now, you've always wanted to go to Ireland, right? You're the least likely one to be watched by Uncle Sam. You've got the time. You're out of college. As a vacationing American college grad you'll have the perfect cover."

"Well, what about the cost?"

"I've already talked to the family," David smiled, "you're funded."

"No, Dave. I don't think I should be the one to go

"What? A chance to go to Ireland, see the old country and do some real good besides? You want to pass this up? Don't tell me no. This is the chance you've been waiting for your whole life. C'mon Mike. Be a hero!" David said smiling with a hand on Michael's shoulder.

"When do you want me to go?"

"Within 30 days. You'll need a passport...I know it's not much time...part of the shipment is traveling by sea. Imported plumbing parts. You'll be carrying the rest of it wrapped in metal foil and paper as first communion gifts and religious items. Your contact man will be Hugh Dorherty. He'll meet you in Dublin and you'll be moved to a safe house in Dundalk. When you get the "holy stuff" to Belfast they'll be put together with the plumbing supplies. The guns will be assembled in Belfast and shipped a few at a time to Derry. After the first shipment of guns gets to Derry, you're to come back. Your cover as an American tourist will only work as long as you keep moving. Don't try to work with any unit operations. You are not to play soldier, understand? Your Yankee accent will stick out like a sore thumb and you'll spend the next 20 years in an internment camp."

"How will they know I'm to be trusted?"

"I've already sent word to them."

"You did? When?"

"Nearly a year ago. I was afraid the U.S. government had a finger on one of our shipments.

"I know they suspect me of gunrunning. I've been back and forth too many times for them not to suspect me. There's a lot more I have to fill you in with so let's get some sleep and we'll talk in the morning. Okay?"

"Yeah. Sure, Dave. I'll be along in a minute."

Dave nodded and went back into the house. Michael stood on the porch. The moonlight gave the front yard and road an amber color. No cars passed down the road to break the stillness It was a very strange summer night, cool, almost like fall. He remembered hearing the geese fly overhead last September. The geese made a great deal of noise when they flew away from their nesting grounds, yet, for some reason, they returned in the Spring in silence.

PART II

Ad'o

It was expected, Mike told himself.   Perhaps Kevin MacKinney couldn't understand it, but he, like so many other Irish Americans, had only heard half the truth.   They were all content to think of Ireland as a land of shamrocks, leprechauns and drunks.   Those who didn't have that impression held a worse one; supplied by British propaganda; that Protestants and Catholics were waging a senseless war of religion on each other.

To Michael, the war was the same as it had been for his great-grandfather, and that was to drive out the English.   The British were simply playing one side against the other.   Divide and conquer.   It was an old imperialist trick they'd used all over the world.   They played the Hindu against the Moslem, the Jew against the Arab, the black against the white and in Northern Ireland they played the Protestant against the Catholic.   The Provisional I.R.A. was opposing the British and not the Protestants.   That was the reason why bombs exploded in British-owned stores and factories and not to kill innocent people as British propaganda tried to lead people to believe.

Out of Boston, Michael's carry-on bag was scanned and he had to walk through the security gates.   He worried about the bags he'd checked through to Dublin.   David had assured him that his other bags wouldn't be searched or x-rayed.   Airport security was single minded to stop highjackings.   "They won't start looking at baggage until some Arab or Cuban plants a bomb in there." David had said.

During the five hour plane ride Michael played a game.   He looked around the cabin and tried to guess who was Irish and was American.   Was there a way to tell by just looking at someone?   Would there be a difference in the look, or perhaps the clothing?   Were there other "tourists" like himself here? Looking out the plane window, the north Atlantic was buried under heavy gray clouds.   They descended beneath the gray and suddenly burst out into the intense green of Ireland's west.   Lines of stone cut the green fields into immense squares.   A few hundred years of backbreaking labor had created those stone walls. The rocky lands of Ireland's west had been turned into productive farms. The British invaders had deemed the west worthless and drove the impoverished Irish there. Generations of people carried the stones and formed those walls. Where there had been nothing but bare rock, the Irish had carried seaweed up the cliffs and created soil. Western Ireland had been the last place to fall to British rule and still maintained the native Irish language. Michael's own family had come from county Kerry. The great Famine of the 1840's had led Michael's ancestors to join the rebellion of the "Young Ireland" movement in 1848. The revolt was crushed and the surviving OShea's had fled to America. They arrived penniless and barely able to walk. The immigrant ships of the day did not provide food for its poor passengers and had less interest in seeing their human cargo survive the voyage than the slave ships did. After all, a slave was worth something and an Irish immigrant would only want to take away an American's job. Michael wondered what his great-great-great- grandfather would have thought of his five hour jump over the ocean. He smiled, swallowed the last of his beer and handed the empty plastic cup to the stewardess.

The plane landed at Shannon Airport. It was a mandatory stop even though Michael's final destination was Dublin. Dublin had it's own airport but the Irish government maintained a "duty-free" shop at Shannon and it was economically wise to make sure the American tourists had plenty of chances to spend their money. The Shannon airport buildings gave Michael a strange feeling. The modernistic look it had was something he had never connected with Ireland. It certainly stood out in the land of mist and stone. There was definitely too much brick and glass. It looked as if it belonged in New York or Chicago.

He felt lost here. The crowds, the very size of the airport building made him feel small. Announcements boomed into the hallways, with a heavy brogue enlacing each word, making even the names of familiar places sound strange and foreign. Shannon airport would be his official port of entry. His bags were rolled unopened through customs. His passport stamped and other than a moment of worry when asked if he had anything to declare, Michael and the guns entered Ireland without incident.

The plane took off again and rose over the Irish countryside. It was only a short hop to the eastern side of the country and Dublin

Michael stepped through the gate into the Dublin Airport. Nearly everyone getting off the place was met by someone. All he knew is that he was to be met by his contact person. Mike looked over the crowd of strange faces. Suddenly a large smiling red-haired man came walking toward him.

"You must be Mike O'Shea?" he said and held Michael's hand firmly and pumped it.

"You've got to be Hugh Dorherty."

"I am. Are you hungry, Mike? Breakfast?"

"Sure."

" I was told you'd have a lot of baggage. Sorry I had to park my van so far away, but you know what they say: if man were meant to fly there'd be more parking space at the Dublin airport."

Mike laughed and started to follow.

"No. Stay here and bring everything curbside and I'll swing by for a pick up, okay? Michael pulled his oversized army duffel bags over to the curb. The "plumbing parts" and "first communion gifts" were heavy but he had wrapped them in his clothing to protect them. He could hear the canvas bags wearing away as he dragged them over the cement. He decided to lift them rather than face the possibility of a rifle barrel falling out on the sidewalk where the Irish police, the Garda, might see it.

Hugh Dorherty pulled up in a rattling green VW van. He slid the side door open and helped Michael pull the bags inside.

For his entire life, Michael had felt and seen himself as Irish, now suddenly as he looked out the window of Hugh Dorherty's van as it cruised down the wrong side of the road, he saw himself as an American in a foreign land. The buildings were different. The road signs were in Gaelic and English. Even the color of the mountains and hills seemed to be a more intensive green than the land at home.

They drove into the center of Dublin, over the O'Connell Street bridge. Michael knew this place. He had read about the

1916 Easter rising. How the Irish had proclaimed independence at the post office and later fired at a company of British Lancers who had been ordered to drive them off on this very street. Later, they passed the four courts and Michael looked up at the Green Dome . "The Helga" was right here on the river Liffey when it shelled the city", Michael said.

"Helga?" repeated Dorerty. "What's that?"

"The British Gunboat that fired its cannons and nearly flattened Dublin."

Dorerty shrugged, "Don't know. I never had much time for history study."

Michael felt disappointed. He was used to Americans not knowing Irish history but here was a member of the I.R.A. who seemed oblivious to his own past.

"We've got a place for you to stay", Dorherty said as he directed the van into a suburban area of the city. "Its my sister's flat. She shares a house with some other people but most of them are away on college holiday right now, so you'll have a room to yourself." The flat was a fairly large home. The Victorian style house had been split into rooming flats.

Michael stepped out of the van and felt a sudden chill of the morning air send a shiver up his spine. He pulled one of the duffel bags up on his shoulder and waddled toward the house under the uneven weight. They hid everything in a storeroom and Michael was invited to sit and eat in the kitchen. Hugh's sister Lana fixed him some toast and eggs. The conversation was friendly. They asked him about his trip and a few questions about Nixon and Watergate. Between snippets of chat, Michael gobbled down the toast. As he took a bite, Michael suddenly caught Lana's eyes watching him. She blushed, then giggled softly.

"Oh, forgive me Michael, you seemed to be enjoying that so much I ..." She turned red again.

Michael noticed her red hair. Her skin was nearly paper white and her eyes were such a soft pale blue that they seemed to light up from within.

"You can get some sleep after you finish eating, Mike" spoke up Hugh. "I'll be driving the van up to Dundalk to prepare things and be back in a day or two."

Tinte'an

They directed Michael to a small room with a single bed. Michael lay down and felt himself drop into a moving sleep. It was as if he were still on the jet, moving into a dark night. He slept through until the next day and awoke to Lana's soft tapping at the door. "Michael, I've a few days off. Would you care to go about with me?"

"Oh, yes", he mumbled. "Can I have a bit of time to clean up? I'll be right down."

"All right." He could hear the smile in her voice. "I'll meet you out front in an hour."

Michael tried to match his clothing to the style he saw on the street the day before. Black jacket, plain dress shirt, jeans. He wanted to blend in with the Irish. He trotted down and out the front door and Lana had a small VW bug idling on the street.

"Where are we off to?" asked Michael.

"Anywhere you want." She replied with a laugh.

"Grafton Street? "

"Oh, lovely choice."

They wandered around Dublin the rest of the day and later visited a pub. She ordered a stout with blackberry currant. Michael sat across from her holding a black pint of stout at a table and found himself lost in her eyes. She could see his stare and her eyes danced away from his and back again playfully.

She was a student studying to be a teacher. Elementary children are so sweet. She had lived in Canada and did some teaching in a Catholic school.

She had loved it but hated being so far away from Ireland and her parents. Her smile would fade only for a second or two as they talked.

The pub had an impromptu band playing some Irish rebel songs. Michael knew the words and they sang along. At closing time, they walked in Dublin's night air. She took his hand as they crossed a street and stood on the railed sidewalk along the river Liffey. Large white ball-shaped street lights on old fashioned pillars were reflected in the water. The scene was beautiful and Michael felt the urge to kiss her. He turned and looked at Lana. Her eyes were searching his face. They moved closer and their lips met warm and wet softness. He held her. He could feel her heart flutter and her breath on his cheek. Dublin, the people passing by, and the world, melted and everything became Lana.

They found their way back to her car and drove back to the house. Lana took Michael into the parlor. Her fingers moved into his hair and she breathed into his left ear, "It's chilly. Would you like me to light a fire?" Michael nodded.

Lana picked up what looked like a brick. "Have you seen this? Its compressed peat. Much nicer than the old boggy stuff. It burns much better." Michael watched her kneel by the shallow fireplace. His eyes traced her silhouette. "Can you smell it?" she asked.

"Yes", replied Michael. "It's sweet, like burning grass". Lana smiled. The firelight danced in the highlights in her hair and her eyes. Michael found himself drawn to her face again.

"The smell of burning peat is in my soul." she said. "Its like being back on our little bit of a farm... It helps me to forget I'm in a city and have to lock my door." "It is the smell of Ireland. Do you feel the connection, Michael?"

Michael took her face in his hands and kissed her. They made love in the soft warm glow of the peat fire and woke embraced , hearing the morning cackle of jackdaws outside the window.

Alainn

Michael worked the toothbrush down and to the back vigorously. He spat out the paste into the sink and stared back up into his own eyes in the bathroom mirror. He smiled and realized how wonderful he felt. If he wasn't in love with this girl whatever else this feeling was, he knew he had never felt it before.

Lana was downstairs and had put together a breakfast for him. He greeted her with a kiss and pulled her tightly to him. "Oh Michael, rest, rest a bit" and pulled away from him. Her face still wore a playful smile. "So tell me, where are your people from, Michael?"

"County Kerry mostly, some from Limerick by way of Canada to the U.S. My grandmother says that the family came over during the famine and were held on Ile Grosse Island in the middle of the St. Lawrence river. The Americans and British Canadians didn't want any more Irish. Rather than face a return to Ireland, disease or starvation on the island, the family planned to escape by swimming. They didn't know which direction the U.S. was so they split into two groups and jumped into the river and swam to both shores. If you can believe the story; one group became American O'Sheas and the other Canadian"

Lana looked at Michael carefully and touched his nose. "I can see the Irish in you but you're something else too...German perhaps?"

Michael smiled, "Oh, you can tell a person's ancestry by looking at them? In the U.S. they call that sort of thing racism..." Lana winced at that. "But you're right Lana", said Michael. We stayed in Irish neighborhoods but the O'Sheas mixed a little like all other Americans. I had a German great-grandmother."

"I thought so."

"Lana would you like to come and visit the States?"

"Oh, don't be thinking you're going to sweep me off my feet and carry me back to America." She was beaming and Michael could see she was flattered.

"My parents would love you, Lana."
"We've only known each other for two days!"

Leann'an si

Michael listed to Lana's soft breathing. He turned on his side and smiled as he studied her.

The morning light filtered into the bedroom through the shade and gave Lana's normally pale skin a gentle orange glow. He touched her hand and held her small delicate fingers. A woman's hand. It seemed to flow as a gentle line from fingertip to arm while a man's hand bulged like a fan at the fingers then narrowed and bulged again at the arm. Lana's hands were beautiful.

Her eyes fluttered and her lips pursed. Michael studied her face. Her red hair curled about on the pillow. He lightly touched the delicate shape of her nose and lips with his finger. Her skin was dotted in freckles. He had noticed that Lana generally didn't wear much makeup. Her pale complexion probably couldn't handle much artificial color.

She turned and her arm went over his shoulder. She snuggled against him and softly kissed his neck. Michael returned her kisses. He could feel her heart beating.

He looked again at her face across the pillow from him. Who was she? It was like she was a member of his family. As if he had known her all his life. She seemed so familiar and yet foreign. Was it her Irishness? He couldn't help but watch her when she walked or moved. Her voice. Her accent seemed more like music than speech. The cadence as she spoke was poetry. He found himself listening to her as he had listened to no other person in his life.

Her face expressed the world to him. There was the color changes in her pale skin, the smile she flashed, the sparkle in her soft blue eyes, the hands that floated up in the air like birds to adjust her hair. Michael absorbed everything about Lana into his soul.

There was no question now about life or destiny. He was meant to be here in Ireland. He was meant to be with this woman at this place at this time.

Michael drifted off to sleep again and awoke to feel Lana's warm, wet kisses on his cheek. She started to hum and then sing softly in his ear.

"I must be dead." Michael said aloud

"Why?" breathed Lana.

"This has to be as close to heaven as a man can get."

Lana smiled and laughed into the pillow.

Michael paused, "Lana, I know how I feel."

She smiled and kissed his cheek. "You are a sweet, handsome American and I am happy to know you, Michael Patrick O'Shea."

A'Clann

Michael walked with Lana holding hands through the Dublin streets. A small blond-haired , blue-eyed girl tugged at Michael's pantleg. Her accent made her request confusing and Michael asked what she wanted.

The girl asked him for money. She was hungry. He reached into his pocket and gave her a handful of coins. Michael suddenly became aware of a large number of children begging as they walked across the O'Connell Street Bridge. Some walked up and asked directly for money and others sat with paper cups. Lana explained that large numbers of children begged on the bridge and were sometimes joined in the evenings by discreetly dressed prostitutes who may have even been their mothers. Dublin, Ireland's capital city and the most prosperous place in the nation was plagued by poverty.

Lana had pointed out the Ballymun area on a drive through the city. It looked very modern. High rises and gray towers had replaced the quaint old neighborhoods. Like the ghetto areas in the States, they simply transferred the poor to newer but soulless housing projects. Looking like rows of ice cube trays standing on end, the area had simply become home for drugs and crime.

Children's playgrounds had been forgotten in the developer's blueprints and now children used abandoned cars as slides and playhouses.

Lana had urged Michael not to talk about the I.R.A. or say political things in the pubs of Dublin. The Dublin press had long portrayed the I.R.A. as criminals and, as a result, Irish nationalism once a thing of great pride had become almost an embarrassment.

Outside Dublin, Irish Republicanism was stronger and the "Jackeens" as Dubliners were called were viewed with some suspicion.

Lana offered to take Michael to visit her sister Mary and her husband Noel. They had a small farm near the Wicklow Mountains. There would not be a meeting with Lana's parents.

Certainly not yet. They would be terrified that Michael would take Lana away to the States. They were also opposed to the I.R.A. and anything connected with it. Hugh's I.R.A. activities had caused him to be banned from the family home

Lana's involvement with the I.R.A. was limited to providing safe houses and an occasional drive of I.R.A. men up to the border. One time, Lana told Michael she had been on a mission filled with I.R.A. operatives. They had rented a bus and traveled North under the guise of being a church choir. They had even spent hours practicing singing religious songs so as to be believable when they crossed the border. She really enjoyed that. She loved to sing. Her brother Hugh had pulled her off the bus before they even reached Dundalk. This was far too dangerous for his baby sister.

Michael looked at her. "I don't blame him. I would never want you anywhere near danger."

Lana smiled. "Oh, so you're my protector now?"

"I wouldn't want anything to happen to you" he replied.

"...And what about you, Michael Patrick O'Shea? Why is it all right for you to do dangerous things, like smuggle guns and not all right for me?"

"What?" Michael was taken aback. "Because, it would break my heart if anything happened to you!"

"Oh? And if something happened to you? How do you think I'd feel?"

"Tell me Lana..." replied Michael. "How would you feel?"

Her eyes suddenly sparked and brimmed with tears. She reached over and took his hand and held it to her cheek. "I think I'd die."

"No. You couldn't. Someone has to be around to tell everyone what a fine fellow I was."

"Don't joke." She smiled and playfully punched his arm.

"I'm not."

"Damn! Now we're going to see my sister and my eyes are red and puffy!"

"They'll think I did something cruel to you."

"Oh, that wouldn't make a good first impression now would it?" she smiled.

Lana did all the driving and Michael caught himself as he nearly walked to the wrong side of the car. With cars on the other side and steering wheels on the other side, Michael felt himself constantly in the wrong place.

They arrived at Noel and Mary O'Neal's home in late afternoon. Michael stepped out of Lana's VW Bug and saw three freckled-faced children peeping at him through the curtains. The curtains suddenly closed as an unseen adult hand slowed their curiosity.

"I imagine they want to see the American that their Aunt is dating." said Michael.

"Oh, more like they're being brats." said Lana.

The front door opened and Noel, a large bald man with a strong handshake greeted him. Mary's hand extended to Michael. Her hands were warm and wet and she had a dish towel over her shoulder. The three children clung to their parents' legs in the doorway.

"This," Mary indicated the two red-haired girls, "is Kerry and this is Breda."

The girls in turn each shook Michael's hand with a hard high pumping action that brought a smile to his face.

"And this is Thomas." Noel said and gave the boy a slight push. Thomas had hair that was nearly midnight black but a complexion as pale as Lana's . The boy tried to give Michael a high five. Something he had undoubtedly seen on television.

"Do you want to see my pony?" Thomas asked.
"Sure." said Michael.

Thomas' face lit up with excitement. "He's very soft and easy to catch! His name is Malarkey!"

"No, Thomas" replied Noel. "They've only just arrived. Later."

Michael could see both Hugh and Lana in Mary's face. Mary was a slightly older and slightly heavier version of Lana. She offered some tea and warm bread. In conversation, Michael listened and watched Lana and Mary match gestures and laughter. It felt good being here. It was warm and welcome

"Did you say your family is from Tipperary?" Mary asked.

"Yes" replied Michael. "But we're originally from county Kerry...You know, the ancestral home."

"Any relation to Kitty O'Shea?" Lana asked smiling.

"The lady who had an affair with Charles Stewart Parnell? I don't think so. The American O'Sheas were away from Ireland by then" answered Michael.

"Besides Mary," added Noel, "O'Shea was her married name. She was cheating on her husband, Captain O'Shea and ruined the reputation of Parnell. He was probably the last man who could have won Ireland's independence peacefully. Sad, what people will give up for love, eh?"

Michael looked over at Lana. "Maybe."

"Maybe?" Lana asked with a sly smile. "Have you any regrets so far?"

"No...not yet" laughed Michael.

"Are you expecting any regrets?"

"I hope not."

Lana leaned over, hugged him and whispered: "Tonight, I'll make sure you'll have no regrets."

The next day, Michael and Lana offered to take the children on an outing. Lana had some favorite walks on a mountain trail. The Wicklow Mountains weren't very high mountains, more like rolling hills and they reminded Michael a little of the Adirondacks. The trail was little more than a goat path. Kerry and Breda walked along close to Lana while the dark-haired Thomas ran ahead and then back every few minutes.

"We'll climb this mountain once but Thomas will do it five times" laughed Michael.

There were few trees but lots of shoulder high bushes. Michael jumped when a dull-eyed sheep came out beside him. There was a splash of bright blue paint on the white wool of the ewe's backside; placed there to mark its owner.

The children cheered when they spotted a large metal cross set into concrete at the top of the mountain.

Lana spun Michael around and pointed. Michael smiled at the view of the lush and beautiful farm field and woodlands below.

Lana took his hand. "Do you see the forty shades of Irish green?"

"There must be at least 40."

Lana looked up into Michael's eyes. "Could you live here Michael?"

He looked over the green patchwork of land down in the valley. "At this moment, I think I could." He held Lana close, feeling her arms about him; her hair blew gently back. Michael kissed her.

All at once the three children giggled.

Priosun

The next day they returned to Dublin. Lana told him to dress warmly and they sipped tea and snacked on soda bread.

"Why dress warmly?" he asked.

"The place is always so damn cold."

"What place?"

"I'm going to 'tourist' you", she said slyly.

"What?"

"We're going to visit Kilmainham jail."

The place had been a British prison and earned an infamous name in Irish history. After Ireland won its independence, the jail was left to fall to ruin. In 1966, it was restored and opened as a museum. Michael had heard stories about Kilmainham since childhood.

The walls were gray limestone and the entranceway was an elaborately carved pattern that resembled a coral reef. Iron bars and a steel door covered the opening and set above the door, fashioned from bronze, was a sculpture of a twisting group of evil looking snakes. The message was very clear. This had once been the entry way to Hell.

The tour guides were very much in favor of Irish Nationalism. Michael was shown the stark cell where the Irish rebel, Wolfe Tone, had cut his own throat with a smuggled razor to escape the British hangman. He saw the room where Robert Emmet had spent his last night on earth after giving an impassioned speech in British court pleading for Ireland's freedom.

Lastly, Michael saw the prison courtyard where the leaders of Ireland's 1916 rebellion were placed against a wall and executed by firing squad.

One of these rebels, James Connelly, had been so badly wounded in the fighting that they had to prop him up in a chair before they shot him.

All Irish heroes, all martyrs, and all very dead.

In the main hall of the prison museum, Michael found the name of a Donal O'Shea on a list of those who were killed in the 1916 rebellion. There was a display cabinet of British Lee Enfield rifles that had been used by both sides in the fighting. Michael looked at the guns and remembered killing a deer in the Adirondacks with an Enfield rifle.

Lana was right when she suggested dressing warmly. The cold limestone walls made this building as cold and damp as a cave. Michael was chilled through and shivered when he finally left Kilmainham jail. The place had moved him.

Imeacht

Hugh had called. Lana was to bring Michael up to Dundalk, near the border. Michael was to meet and discuss the needs of the I.R.A. for future shipments of arms. In a few days, he would return to his life in the States.

On the drive north, Lana had asked him to stay in Ireland, but Michael knew there were no jobs. She reminded him that he could live on the "dole", but it wasn't possible. Michael couldn't live on government handouts. He asked her to come to America and Lana finally agreed to a visit.

"Michael, you have no idea what it means to an Irish person to immigrate."

"What? Lana, I'm descended from Irish immigrants. Of course I know."

"No you don't. Michael, you only know it from one side. You don't know what it does to the people you leave behind. If I left, it would kill my parents."

"No, No, this is the modern age of jet travel. You wouldn't be on an 1840's coffin ship. You could return home in a day by plane."

"You really can't understand, can you? Michael, America is your home and everyone there is like you. Even though you're Irish. You see it isn't the distance, or the jet...It is the leaving. "When we leave Ireland, we break the hearts of our family and we lose part of ourselves."

Michael watched the windshield wipers clean the soft Irish mist away. He looked over to her. "So Lana, are we to have a great and tragic love? Never to get together, like Romeo and Juliet? Tristan and Isulde?" (She smiled.) "Sonny and Cher?" (She laughed.)

"Well, Michael, great heroes often have tragic and lost loves. Did you know that?"

An mhair teoil

Lana's sister's boyfriend owned the safe house in Dundalk. He had been employed by the Guinness company and they had sent him all over the world. His walls were covered with kangaroo hides, African masks, and souvenirs of his travels. Tom Connolly put Lana and Michael in a back room on the upper floor of his house.

Michael offered to make dinner and hiked down to street to the local shop. Irish money consisted of large bills that didn't fit well into an American wallet and heavy coins that filled his pockets. The Irish punt was worth nearly double the dollar on the exchange. Every small purchase produced a handful of coins and he felt weighted down by them.

Michael had planned to make a stew that night. When he heard the lady store clerk speaking Gaelic to a customer he decided to try some of the language he had learned at home. Michael looked at the young girl clerk.

"Dia duit", he said. "Ba Mhaith liom feoil." The girl stared at him and suddenly laughed.

Michael was embarrassed. "Did I say it wrong?" he asked.

"No, no.", the girl replied. "Your Irish was fine but I've never heard it with an American accent. I didn't mean to laugh. How much beef did you want?" Michael, red faced, finished his shopping in English.

Ireland spoke English except for some small areas on the Aran Islands and in the west. The schools taught Gaelic and the street signs were all in English and Irish but English, the language of the enemy, was what you normally heard in Ireland. The Irish who could speak Irish spoke Irish to each other. Michael felt American.

Michael spooned the stew into 3 stone bowls. Lana and Tom carried the kitchen table out into his little backyard garden. They ate their meal there among the flowers. "Its quite good, Michael" said Tom. Lana echoed the same.

"I don't often use beef." Michael replied. "My Cousin David and I used to go deer hunting in the fall. Its really how I make venison stew

"You hunt deer?" Lana asked.

"Yes."

"That's terrible. How can you kill a helpless animal."

"Oh Lana, they'd face a much more horrible death in the wild...eaten alive by dogs, starving to death..."

Tom looked thoughtful "I've never killed an animal, don't think I could, but it wouldn't be hard at all to point a gun at another human being. I have no problem at all feeling angry at evil men."

Teolai

Michael woke the next morning with soft warm kisses covering his face. Lana had to leave for Dublin. No, she never crossed into the North; not since she was a child when it was so much cheaper to shop there. Now they avoided travel there. "Here's a picture in case you forget me." (Wet tears) "Good-bye Michael. I'll see you back in Dublin in a few days. I'll see if I can book a flight back with you. You can show me America. Michael, I love you. I still won't let you drag me to live in the States, but I'll let you keep trying to convince me." A long lingering deep kiss. She left him alone in bed, glowing from her warmth.

O'thuaidh

Hugh Dorerty was downstairs at the breakfast table. He had heated up some leftover stew and passed a bowl over to Michael. "Stew is always best the second day, isn't it?" "Yes" replied Michael.

"Getting along with Lana?" asked Hugh suddenly.

"Oh, yes."

"Good. She seems to like you."

"That's good. I like her too."

"We'll be crossing into the north today. You probably won't need your passport but the border guards may demand to see it just to be a pain."

"Your cousin David knew us. I know he'd be here if the U.S. Government wasn't keeping such a close watch on him. This is all new to you. We want to bring you in only to share information and then send you back. We have needs and the supplies need to be kept flowing. They want you to be a contact man. Eyewitness to the inside. Are you ready for this?"

"Hugh" replied Michael. "I can't wait."

Hugh Dorherty and Michael drove toward the border in an old blue Volvo. They stopped at a roadside "money exchange" and converted some Irish punts into British pounds. They continued the drive along the green Irish hills. The land between Northern Ireland and the Irish republic gave no signs of its dual nature. Ulster and the Irish Republic were exactly the same as far as Michael's eyes could see. It was the concrete walls, barbed wire and warning signs that told him he was about to enter British-controlled territory. The first sign was in black and yellow: Caution Border Crossing. No Photography. Stop On Command. A second sign was in black and white: Switch Off Lights. There was a barricade beyond the signs made of stacked cement block that stood about 10 feet high. Razor wire stretched out on the top of the barrier and ran up the hills on either side of the road. A machine gun emplacement was set into a concrete tower above the road and the machine gun tracked each car as it moved through the check point. A long red and white pole raised and then lowered as each car took its turn going through

There were several soldiers with machine guns visible walking along the side of the wire fencing. Michael could see a British flag flying in the distance. Hugh eased the blue Volvo forward . A soldier in a green uniform and helmet came toward the driver's side of the car. Michael could see a machine gun in the man's hands. This was one of them, one of the oppressors of his people, his family, about to come face to face with the enemy.

The soldier bent at the waist and his face came into view. Michael was shocked to see a pimply-faced boy who looked younger than himself. Michael studied him. The kid had a serious face but he looked like someone had taken away his favorite toy. This was a British soldier?

"Where are you going?" he said flatly. His teeth were crooked and yellow.

"Belfast."

"Citizenship?"

"Irish and U.S."

The soldier looked over at Michael and pointed at him with his chin.

"Passport?"

Michael fumbled for his passport. He passed it over to Hugh to the soldier's hands. The boy's eyes flicked quickly over Michael's papers and then glanced at his picture and then back at Michael.

"Sightseeing, Yank?" a hint of sarcasm in his voice.

Michael looked back at the soldier. "Visiting friends" said Hugh in an impertinent tone. The boy soldier's face turned red with frustration. He looked into the cab of the car. "Buckle your fucking seat belts!" He shouted. Hugh and Michael quickly obeyed. Buckles clicked. "Move on!"

The Volvo eased over the concrete rise at the gate the tailpipe scraping as they moved on to the road to Belfast.

"Guess he didn't like my attitude." Hugh muttered.

"Or he didn't like tourists" replied Michael.

Belfast was an amazing place. Michael had seen many pictures of the city on the news. Everything looked calm, modern, even prosperous. It wasn't the war ravaged city Michael expected. But the war mentality , the war atmosphere was everywhere.

They drove into the city center and Hugh steered the Volvo into a parking garage. Two blue uniformed men came quickly to the side of the car. "Get out. Open the boot and the bonnet and stand there."

They had a hand cart with a mirror mounted on it and directed it under the Volvo. The men looked into the trunk and even into the engine. Hugh smiled slightly as the men gave permission for them to be on their way. From the parking garage, Hugh and Michael made their way to the street.

Michael looked up from downtown Belfast at the towering green-domed City Hall. Hanging between the marble pillars was a great banner. "Ulster says No!" "Ulster is right." "Ulster will fight." Hugh looked at it in disgust. "Ulster says No! No freedom, no peace, no equal rights for nationalists." and then suddenly, with a smile, he added: "Don't you just hate negative people? Years ago we tried to bring some nationalist parts of Ulster into the republic and they put a banner up there that said "Not an inch!" Course now the bastards went metric so they'll have to find more space for "Not a centimeter!"

Michael laughed.

"Downtown Belfast is generally considered neutral territory, but you'll still see plenty of soldiers and police here." Businessmen in suits. Ladies with children shopping. Policemen in blue with bullet proof vests and soldiers in khaki green walked the streets of Belfast. The skyline was Victorian but filled with new construction.

Michael marveled, "There's a war going on here?"

"Belfast is booming in more ways than one." joked Hugh.

They had lunch at a store cafeteria. Hugh made two telephone calls and they returned to the car.

The city of Belfast was divided like East and West Berlin. The Loyalist/Protestant neighborhoods were decorated with red, white and blue and British flags , they appeared to Michael to be only slightly nicer than the Nationalist/Catholic neighborhood which flew the Irish tricolor. They were divided by walls and wire. In some cases piles of red brick had been heaped up in the middle of the street or rusted burned-out cars had been used as walls.

There were ruins and bombed out buildings and British rubber-wheeled Saracen tanks rumbled through the streets.

They passed by a fortress of concrete blocks, TV cameras, motion detectors and razor wire that revealed it was a neighborhood police station. They didn't see any violence but evidence of the violence was everywhere. They drove down Donegal Street turning after a while. Hugh pulled the car into a small lot behind a block of red brick flats. They walked up three floors, down a dark hallway and into the flat of Larus Duddy.

Duddy was a squat little man, a living stereotype of the gnarled Irishman, about sixty years old Michael guessed. He wore wire-type glasses that hooked the rims of his ears, making then appear pulled forward. He met them in his undershirt and fed Hugh and Michael some tea and lukewarm soup.

Duddy was the education officer. The I.R.A. had long ago realized that ignorance was a great enemy and each battalion had one officer assigned to this duty. Since Michael was about to enter their world, Larus Duddy was assigned to instruct him.

"We have plenty of manpower." Duddy said. "60% of Catholic Belfast is unemployed. Unhappy, disenfranchised and very aware of their oppression. What we need is a way to keep our forces armed. We have a very large number of people who are I.R.A. auxiliaries and trained to defend themselves and their areas. Small boys and girls at play watch everything. Their mothers can spread alarms by banging dustbin lids and pots and we have armed watchmen to shoot back and enforce laws.

We have active soldiers who do our offensive proactive fighting, bombing and assassination. They're generally the ones that get written about in the papers

We also have "sleeper" units in Britain. They are assigned to emigrate to Britain, get jobs and blend in. They stay out of politics and anything Irish. After a few years they are "activated" by a telephone call and a Gaelic code word. The assignment or target is taken and the British have no way to find our agents.

Ours is the war of the flea against the elephant. We sting, hit and run. We could never hope to match our strength against the British Army but we can harry them to despair. Ours is a war of attrition. We will slowly wear down the British will to hold on to Northern Ireland.

Our bombing campaign is aimed at the enemy financial interests. We will make Ulster "unprofitable." We will make normal government operations impossible so Ulster will be "ungovernable".

"Our contacts in the international community give us support politically and financially. We have no doubt that we will win. Our cause is just, right and natural. The British are our oppressors and while they have the strength to fight, they lack our will. A British soldier must be assigned here. He has no freedom to choose. He is supported by involuntary taxation from an apathetic population. The average Britt is far more interested in the newest Princess Diana gown than how many soldiers we killed. "

"Now the I.R.A. is made up of unpaid volunteers. Our soldiers are supported voluntarily by the people. Food, shelter, weapons, even medical supplies and hidden hospitals (The Green Cross); everything is free and voluntary.

<u>Fardarrig</u>

Duddy stopped talking for a moment and looked at Michael. Michael returned the gaze. There was the sound of a car outside, its tires hissing a wet spray in the rainy air. Duddy was watching Michael's reaction to his narration on the I.R.A.

"Do you know where you are Michael."

Michael nodded. "In Belfast."

"Yes, Belfast, but we're at a crossroads in history. The troubles here in Ireland have been economic as well as political. Thousands of young people leave every year. Our brightest and best board jets instead of ships now and leave. There are no jobs in Ulster for Nationalists and there is no hope of work for them unless we win their political rights." He ran his hand through his thinning hair.

"Whole villages have lost all their young people. They go to England, Canada or the States. If they would stay, we might win this war by increasing our population."

"What do you mean," asked Michael. "The Nationalists could vote themselves free of the Brits if they had cnough people?"

"Oh no," replied Duddy, "I know the Brits say they'd respect the democratic system but that's a lie. I'm not that naive to believe they'd let us win our freedom peacefully. Look at all the countries around the world that Britain occupied. There is hardly a one that didn't have a bloodbath before the Brits decided to 'respect the democratic wishes of the people'.
I do believe that if we could convince the young people to stay that we would be able to end this fight. The only problem is it might take twenty or thirty years. It might take too many more lives, too." He paused. "My son died out on the streets back in 1969. He was just nineteen and only carrying a sign, protesting, asking for equal rights for Catholics. They just fired into the crowd and he was gone...." Duddy's eyes glistened. He took off his glasses and wiped his face with the back of his hand

Michael saw that this war had scarred Duddy and probably many others. You didn't see many scarred or crippled people on the street. Most injuries would be invisible, on the inside, and far beyond any hope of healing.

Duddy looked up at Michael. "The Official I.R.A. helped us and then backed off so we formed our own Provisional Irish Republican Army and we've been fighting the Brits ever since."

Michael wondered at it all. He'd grown up in an Irish neighborhood and been immersed in Irish culture and history but he was only now beginning to understand the people he had always thought of as his own. He had an American coloration to everything. The Irish Americans could have their Nationalist fight without personal loss or injury. Sharing the pride of being American, a nation that had never really been defeated, with Ireland, a nation which had never really known victory.

The next day Duddy continued his lecture, "We do not recognize the British right to rule us and we enforce our own laws in our own areas. We don't have prisons but we do have courts. A thief might get a warning the first time, a beating the second time and have his kneecap shot off on the third offense. Our soldiers have their own court martial procedure. An accused soldier is judged by three members of equal rank and the accused may defend himself, call witnesses, etc. A sentence of death must be ratified by the Adjutant Commander." Duddy stopped for a moment and lit a cigarette, "Have you any questions?"

"Yes, where are the guns I brought?"

Hugh laughed, "In the Volvo. The metal parts are inside the floor boards and I put the gun stock inside the door panels." " I was only worried about getting caught when they put mirrors underneath the car at the parking garage."

Duddy smiled.   "The Volvo changes license plates and colors on a regular basis. The British Army still hasn't worked it out yet. We do have to keep changing drivers."

Hugh turned to Michael. "Its a bit like being 007, isn't it?" Michael smiled and Duddy looked at him with narrowed eyes. "What is it that brings you into this; Yank?" Are you playing soldier or spy?"

Michael chaffed at this, "My family has been sending money and arms for years, for generations. We were working for Irish freedom even before there was an I.R.A. Ever since they drove my family off our lands."

"A returning noble, eh? Ha! I never met an American yet whose ancestors weren't at least Earls. To hear them talk, you'd think only kings and their courts went to America instead of the trash and cowards who ran away when Ireland needed them. Well, welcome! Welcome home avenging son! Welcome home!

Michael fell silent, angry. "All right! I think he's proved he's Davy's cousin, " said Hugh.

Duddy gave out a half-smile. "He's got the same hanged pride, but if David Murphy says he is to be trusted then he is to be trusted."

Hugh turned to Michael. "We use the public clubs for meetings. There's drink and music and the background noise makes it impossible for British listening devices and wire taps to sort out the conversations. Since its a neighborhood place, they can't get in agents without them being recognized as strangers. We'll bring you in tonight, introduce you to the unit commanders, and they can fill you in on our needs. When you go back to the States you can let them know you talked directly to the men in the field. That way they can see exactly what all their dollars have been doing in this country, eh?"

Tuairisc

Michael left the Belfast safe house and walked about the neighborhood. There were few people about and the area seemed peaceful. A few dogs barking, some music from the corner pub. He let his feet direct his wandering. When his shoes started to hurt, he selected a pub and went in.

"Pint of stout please" Michael asked the barman.

"You a yank?" someone called from behind him.

Michael heard the voice. The Northern Irish accent had a hollow sound to it. It was almost Scottish. It was Irish like the Dublin accent only with a resonance. It was an Irish voice that sounded like someone was shouting into an empty rain barrel.

Michael turned to see who had addressed him. He saw that the man was a short chubby fellow with thin red hair and a nose to match. However, it was the picture on the wall behind him that let Michael know he was in the wrong place. There was a portrait of King William of Orange on the wall. Michael had walked into a Unionist pub.

"Yes, I am." Michael replied. He covered his nervousness and took a sip of his stout.

"I thought so. I heard enough Yank talk in the cinema and on the tellie to recognize it right off. Only been fooled twice. Canadians and Australians sound a lot like Americans. My name's Willie Hutton."

He extended his hand out at an angle for Michael to shake. Michael took it and the man looked into him. He was looking Michael right in the eyes and holding onto his hand. Was he on to something or just a friendly fellow trying to engage Michael in conversation?

"See now" Willie said, "we don't get many foreigners to hear our side of things."

"Things?" asked Michael.

"You know about the troubles here in Ulster."

"Yes."

"The American press is very pro-Taig. They never hear our side."

Michael smiled. "I'd be interested in listening to that

"Well," smiled Willie, "we're the majority here in Ulster. In a democratic system it is the will of the majority that rules right? You Americans vote for a president. It's the majority that decides who runs America, right? The majority of people here support the union with Britain and we want to remain British." Michael nodded.Willie took a swallow of his stout. He suddenly sang:

> "If guns were made for shooting,
> then skulls were made to crack.
> You've never seen a better Taig
> than with a bullet in his back!"

Michael tried not to show his shock.

Willie went on: "Many of us are descendants of people who settled in Northern Ireland back in the 1500's. That's before the first settlers in America arrived. People call us invaders like we just got here. Ulster is as much our home as anyone else's. Think of it, would you give America back to the Indians? Why should we give anything to the Taigs."

Michael thought for a moment then took a deep swallow of his drink.

"I suppose it all depends on how you look at the issue. You're a majority in Ulster but in the rest of the Island of Ireland you're the minority."

Willie appeared somewhat upset at Michael's reply.

"Well now, that's why we broke free of the Taig-republic so we wouldn't be a minority."

"Yes. I suppose you're right." said Michael.

"There now," smiled Willie, "when you get back to the States you tell them that. Then maybe you Yanks will stop buying guns for those murderers."

Michael finished his pint and made a discreet exit.

Aire duit

"Don't ever do that again!" shouted Hugh after learning about Michael's nighttime wandering.

"You could get killed. People disappear here when they walk into the wrong area. ...Are you stupid or crazy?"

"Sorry, I didn't even realize I'd crossed into another area." Michael replied.

"You're in a war zone. It might look like a neighborhood but it's a bleeding war! You don't go wandering! Ever!"

Duddy has sat calmly looking out the window and listening to Hugh blast Michael. He smiled slightly and then cleaned his glasses on his shirt. Duddy pointed to the street. "Perhaps Michael is bored. Part of the life of the I.R.A. is sitting and waiting and experiencing absolute terror when something finally does happen... Look here."

Michael and Hugh looked out the window.

"They're spying on us." said Duddy. "See that lorry over there, the one for the nappy service? Michael, for you, the truck with the diaper service."

"That pretty little girl that had a baby without a father, Margaret Maddison, had a look inside when she brought the nappy pail out. She says the inside is paneled. It's different from the old delivery truck and they've a new driver, too. Look carefully at the sides. See the small vent openings near the top? I'll bet they have listening devices and cameras in there. They're listening in on conversations in each house and photographing people on the street."

"The cheek of them." stammered Hugh.

"I've an idea. Michael, would you like to help?" Duddy asked.

Michael smiled. "Sure."

Bua

Michael sat close to 17-year-old Margaret Maddison as she breast-fed her infant son. They watched the street for the diaper delivery truck.

"That's it" she said and touched his hand. She apparently had keener hearing than Michael, as she heard the distinctive rumble and gear grind of the vehicle that made regular trips through her neighborhood.

Margaret put her son down in his crib and took one bucket of soiled diapers and water, and Michael took the other. They opened the door and stepped out into the afternoon sunshine, and waited on the street of red brick row houses.

The driver got out smiling. "You've two pails of nappies for me, eh, Maggie?"

"Yes, I do." said Margaret. "But you'll not be charging me for either."

"What?" The driver's jaw dropped and he tilted his cap back.

"I said you'll not charge me for this." Margaret repeated.

Michael tried to wear a look of anger on his face and held Margaret's hand as if they belonged together.

"Why won't you pay me might I ask?" demanded the driver.

"You charged me double last week" replied Margaret.

"I did not." the driver shouted red faced.

"Then prove it! Show me your receipts." demanded little Margaret.

Michael folded his arm across his chest and tried to look intimidating."

"Who's he?" the driver pointed to Michael.

"Me boyfriend, Robert, and he'll kick your arse if you dare try to charge me double again." snapped Margaret.

Michael smiled and winked at the driver, pointed at the toe of his shoe and said in his best imitation Belfast accent: "Yer arse!"

The driver was furious. "Don't threaten me! I'll show you the bleeding receipts and then I'll kick your arse!" He started flipping through his receipt book.

A group of teenage boys in the meanwhile had taken the diaper pails and quietly climbed up to the top of the delivery van.

The driver heard them just as the boys poured the contents of both buckets down the roof air vent into the hidden panel room.

There was a sudden pounding and screaming. The panel inside the truck exploded open and two British soldiers burst out of the back end of the truck covered and reeking of infant feces.

A crowd of boys had gathered and began jeering and hurling the soiled diapers at the soldiers.

The driver and the two soldiers began to run.

"Don't ever come back here again or we'll wipe your arses!"

One diaper hit a soldier right in the back of the head and the crowd erupted in laughter.

"Take some more shite!" someone shouted then threw another diaper. "Here! You forgot these!"

The driver and the two soldiers were on full run down the street now. Michael opened the inside of the truck and began smashing the cameras and recording equipment. He stood in the back of the truck turned, and began to rip the recording tape in front of the crowd that had gathered. They cheered. Michael smiled and bathed in the glory of the moment.

Ta'se'ag ba'isteach

It was raining in Belfast. Rain with a wind behind it. Michael looked out and saw what he believed had to be actual sheets of water falling from the sky. It fell with a spattering sound on the brick and stone city. The few people who raced by had pulled down hats, pulled up collars and dancing battered umbrellas.

Michael felt the warmth of Duddy's small electric heater at his back and involuntarily shivered.

He was bored. In Dublin, he had felt free to wander and he had Lana. He missed her and wanted to telephone her just to hear her voice. He couldn't of course. There couldn't be any links between this house and her. The British had agents in Dublin and if there were any connection between the I.R.A. and Lana that might be the end of her.

Telifis

Michael found himself both amused and bored by television in Northern Ireland. There was an abundance of 'educational' programming intermixed with 'news' (all carefully censured) and a lot of reruns of old American TV shows like "I Love Lucy" and "Star Trek".

He found most of his time in Belfast was just sitting around waiting to hear something. The show today, however, was "Sunday Issues" and there was an actual debate going about real events in Northern Ireland.

Politician A was speaking about the benefits of British rule and how all Ulstermen should be happy the British Army was here in Northern Ireland controlling things so the blessing of British democracy could continue.

"The Provisional I.R.A. propaganda would lead us to believe that Northern Ireland is under "colonial rule". When in fact, it is part of Great Britain and our legally elected representatives, elected by the majority of the population, wish to remain part of Great Britain. Ulster is hardly an oppressed third world country." said Politician A.

The camera turned to Politician B who was supposed to be representing the liberal point of view.

"I will agree that the P.I.R.A. stands against liberal democratic practices as it threatens their total control of the people. They certainly wouldn't want to have people happy with the status quo.

The Provisional I.R.A. has adopted a leftist stance only as a ruse. They have seen their sources of funding in the U.S. drying up and so they have begun to associate with communists, socialist and terrorist nations.

They hardly believe in socialism. If they wanted to be communists they would support the Official I.R.A. which is openly Marxist."

Politician A replied, "So you're saying the I.R.A. is rather like the Mafia in the U.S.?"

Politician B: "Oh no! The Mafia is only interested in money and power. They have no political agenda

Politician A: "Still the I.R.A. controls money and drugs, robs banks. They are just criminals to me."

Politician B: "No. That's just like equating the two because the Mafia and the I.R.A. both use guns. Besides, we all know that the Mafia encourages drug use and the I.R.A. punishes anyone who brings drugs into their areas. In fact, I find it quite ironic that there is so little true crime in Northern Ireland. A criminal cannot mug an old lady, sell drugs or rob a home because the I.R.A. won't stand for it. Criminals have their kneecaps blown off! If it wasn't for the shootings and bombings this would be a very peaceful country indeed. I believe the root cause of our problems is the poverty in this land.

Unemployment in Northern Ireland is the highest in Europe. In some areas here 80% of the young men have no jobs and are easily seduced by groups like the I.R.A."

Politician A replied: "I'd never believe that. Read the newspapers. Anyone who really wants employment can find work. We simply have a large portion of our people who would rather collect money on the "Bru."

Michael turned to Duddy, "The Bru?", he asked.

"The dole. Welfare." Duddy replied.

Politician A continued: "Look at how many people can afford to send their children to the Gaelic speaking part of Ireland every summer to learn a totally useless language. They use government support monies to pay to have their children become proficient in a dead language."

Politician B: "Would you object if they were learning Latin?"

Politician A: "Well, of course, I wouldn't object to the study of Latin. The study of Latin wouldn't encourage a separate national identity."

Politician B: "Doesn't everyone in Northern Ireland act as if they have a different national identity from the rest of what we call the "United Kingdom"? The Ulster Defense Association is just a loyalist version of the I.R.A. that claims it will fight to remain British even if they have to fight Britain.

Politician A: "Well there is the supreme irony isn't it? Here is Northern Ireland. We have the Ulster Defense Association killing Irish Nationalists to force them to love the British government and the Irish Republican Army killing British loyalists to make them love the Irish Republic."

The two politicians laughed.

Michael changed the channel. Since it was Sunday, religious programming was on. Now he found himself watching the Rev. Dr. Ian Paisley preaching his anti-Catholic pro-unionist venom. The prayers of Dr. Paisley were rantings that were more like a long list of demands on God than soulful requests. Michael shook his head in disgust.

Duddy turned off the T.V. and handed Michael a book written by Gerry Adams.

Seo e m'athair

Hello Dad,

I thought I'd compose a short letter to you while I wait in Belfast.

There is so much I'd love to tell you but I can't, until I get back to the States. You never know who will read the letter or listen in on the phone in Northern Ireland.

I just want you to know I'm working very hard to make the family proud.

I met a wonderful girl in Dublin, and I can't wait to have you meet her.

Love,

Michael

Meaniche

Michael heard a low rumbling sound. Thunder? Thunderstorms were very rare in Ireland. No. It was a cracking sound. Gunshots! His heart was pounding. He looked up and down the street almost pressing his face against the glass. More shots. A small blue Ford raced up the street. Then there was the quiet and the rain.

Belfast quickly became an ordinary place again. Was that life in Belfast? Boredom followed by moments of extreme terror?

Suddenly, Michael felt the earth shake. He felt himself involuntarily jump. There was the roar of an explosion. Michael again looked out the window and saw rubble littering the roadway. A bomb had gone off.

Duddy opened the door to the room a crack.

"Stay put." He said and Michael nodded. A few minutes later a fire truck and ambulance flew up the street sirens wailing.

Michael stared out the window as bodies were loaded in the ambulance. Raindrops flowed down the window glass slowly. There had been fighting and someone had certainly died. Michael had been close to it but not close enough to be hurt.

His fingertips touched the cold glass of the window pane.

"Jesus Christ. This has to end." He said.

Michael in his imagination saw a coffin covered in the Irish tricolor carried through the street and two small children with tears in their eyes throwing a handful of earth on their father's grave.

<u>Failte</u>

That night in the club, Michael felt elated. He was finally inside. He was in and surrounded by the I.R.A. and he was being welcomed as one of them. Commanders and titles were incidental. Michael largely heard only first names and with the volume of the music and talk conversations were lips to ear. No listening device or wire tap could ever pick up what was being said.

"Fully automatic weapons. Shotguns and hunting rifles are better than nothing but we've got to have at least as good as the Tommys."

"M16's and AK47's."

"Missiles to shoot down helicopters."

"There has to be a way to bring in weapons and ammunition on a grand scale...no more smuggling in a few weapons...we should bring in a ship full.

Michael nodded, shook hands and listened. A song came up: "A Nation Once Again" and suddenly the room went into a chorus. Arms went up in the air and the crowd swayed to the music. Michael noticed people in different groups held fingers up, some one, others two and still others three fingers.

"What are they doing?" Michael shouted into Hugh's ear. "Its for the battalion they're in. Belfast has 3 battalions. They're singing for their own battalion number trying to out sing each other."

When the song ended a round faced man with a red nose climbed up on a table. He held up two fingers and shouted "Two! Two! Ado. The winner is two tonight. Tonight we have a raffle for the widows and orphans' fund. One of the interned prisoners made this." He held up a hand-carved wooden harp. "We're offering it as a prize tonight. It has only cotton strings so its just to look at. You can't play it. Its for the widows and orphans and made by one of our own interned men. You can buy a chance, one pound, one chance. For the Nationalist widows and orphans."

People moved forward to buy a ticket. Michael and Hugh each bought chances. Some of the unit commanders that Michael had met bought dozens of chances. O'Brien, Gilmore and McDaid held up handfuls and challenged their men to match them.

The drawing was held only a few minutes later. The red nosed round faced man called out the numbers 5-7-8. Hugh turned to Michael "Shit! I won!" He trotted to the table with his ticket in the air. "Christ! I never win anything! I won!" He shouted.

Hugh put the wooden harp on his shoulder and pretended to play. The group laughed and cheered.

Hugh showed it off. Michael could see it was an Irish harp probably carved as a copy of the one on the Irish coins. The interned prisoner must have spent hundreds of hours on it to create such beautiful detail out of a couple of prison 2x4 boards.

The harp was placed in the center of the table and Michael found himself seated with the 3 battalion commanders.

It was a dream. He was here in Ireland, working with and talking with the leaders of the I.R.A. The wooden symbol of Ireland was there on the table. They were like the warriors of the Red Branch of Irish Mythology. Sitting in the modern equivalent of an ancient mead hall. He felt as he had felt as a boy. He felt heroic...like Cuchulain...like Emmet...like Kennedy. The club was filled with smoke and talk.

A Unit commander named McDavit, leaned forward to the center of the table and motioned for the others to listen. Michael and the others brought their heads in the hear and Michael imagined a great secret was about to be revealed.

"A member of the I.R.A. was captured and thrown into a British internment camp." said McDavit with a smile. " His poor old father wrote to him saying: 'Dear son, I don't know what to do. With you in prison I've no one to help me dig up the north field to plant the potatoes' . The son quickly writes back from the British Prison Camp: 'Da, don't dig up the North field because thats where I buried all the guns for my I.R.A. unit! The lad's father writes back and says that hundreds of British soldiers showed up and dug up the entire North field looking for the guns. The son writes back and says: "Now, you can plant the potatoes!" The group exploded in laughter. Hugh was ready to leave and told Michael it was time. They stepped out the back door. The air felt cool and clean after the beer and smoke-filled club.

"So what do you think?" Hugh asked. The wooden harp rested on his shoulder and suddenly Michael was suddenly aware of a look of horror on Hugh's face.

"Christ!"

"What's wrong?"

"Shut up-Get down!" Hugh hissed.

"What?

"There was a fucking red laser targeting dot right on your forehead."

"Where'd it come from!"

"British soldier up on top of the building. Cross the street. Christ, how did he get in here? One thing's certain. He's not alone. Here, take my harp. Stay here. I can't open the door or he'll see me in the door light. I'll go around to the front and warn everyone. They're probably here in force to round us all off to the internment camps."

Hugh crawled forward, stood up and softly took a few steps and then ran toward the front of the building.

The soldier must have seen the wooden harp and thought it was a gun. Michael stayed tucked down along the door steps. His left hand holding the wooden harp and his right hand and cheek pressed against the stone steps.

"Michael" a voice hissed. "Michael, go this way." It was Duddy. The old man was bent down and pointing toward an alley. Michael spun to his feet and softly ran down the alley, the harp still tucked under his arm. Michael looked back over his shoulder catching a glimpse of Duddy. There was a beaming smile on his face.

What the Hell could that have meant? Michael heard gunshots and felt himself jump with the intensity of the noise. He walked on through the alley. There were some soldiers in front of a store across the street. He stopped, remaining in the darkness of the alley, back from the streetlights.

One of the soldiers pointed in his direction. They had seen him! Michael turned to run, dashing through the alleyway, flinging garbage cans over behind him. The sound of soldiers' feet coming closer. He could hear them kicking cans out of their path. Michael ran, heading for the light on the other side. One blazing light at the end of the darkness.

"Halt!"

He kept running, heart pounding, out of breath, frightened. Suddenly, pain shot through him, his leg fell out from under him. He came crashing, clutching his leg, to the ground. Garbage cans spilled, burying him. A muffled explosion roared into his ears making them ring. The soldiers' feet slowed. He could see them, legs, ugly boots, baggy pants, dark helmeted men standing above him.

"Looks like a fucking angel!" A soldier joked.

Michael realized he'd fallen into the trash pile still holding the wooden harp.

"Get up!"

What? They'd shot him and now they want him to get up? He felt his leg. There was no wound. A rubber bullet?

"Get up!"

They dragged him from the ground and threw him against the wall.

"Arms and fingers spread! Legs apart! On yer toes! Knees bent!" Hands slapped his jacket, legs, under his arms and pockets.

They pulled him out of the alley into the lights. Michael caught only a quick glimpse of the harp, left behind in the trash pile. He walked in a daze, more carried along than under his own power. Down the street under the lights he could see an armored truck coming closer. The steel doors banged open. They pushed him into the dark opening and slammed the metal door behind him.

Instantly, the carrier jerked forward, throwing Michael to the floor. The car was moving down William Street. He could feel the low rumble of the engine through the floor. He tried to count the turns as the carrier swayed by corners. Though it didn't matter. He knew where he was being taken. The barracks. For interrogation.

The carrier slowed down now, as it passed over a concrete rise, then eased to a stop. Michael got to his feet. Standing in the darkness he could hear voices outside.

The steel doors burst open. Light exploded in on him. Two soldiers stood outside in the gray night haze, pointing rifles at him. The barrack lights glared all around.

He was hauled out and thrown into a room. The walls were white, no furniture of any kind, no windows, nothing but blank wall, roof and floor. A heavy wood door closed behind him and locked. A single light bulb hung above his head covered with a cage and steel mesh. He was alone. The silence unnerved him. What would be coming now?

He had information, important information. British soldiers were known in Ireland for torture. He remembered stories of the "Black and Tans". British soldiers who terrorized Ireland so ruthlessly in the 1920's that those who later wrote history books compared them to Nazi Germany's Gestapo.

There had been torture here in Northern Ireland in recent years as well. Men had been left crippled and blinded by British soldiers and police. The Red Cross had seen it. The stories had been in the papers.

The possibility of being tortured? How do you brace yourself for something like this? In the movies, the hero always resists. They ask questions and the hero makes jokes. Of course in the movies no one is really in pain. Pain?

How do you get ready to withstand pain? God. He'd heard the British also used drugs. They say though that drugs won't work very quickly if you fight them. That would mean that in order to get information from him within a short time, they would have to use some kind of torture.. He tried to remember what the Red Cross said they had been using. Something about electric shocks and burnings. Oh, and that picture, Christ! That man's face!

They said he had been beaten with nightsticks. Well, if they tried to beat him, he would fight! He'd show them he wasn't afraid of them, even if they killed him, they'd not break him. But...what if they did? What if they did something to make him talk. They'd have O'Brien and Duddy, Hugh and the others. (Duddy? Why had he smiled like that?) They'd have all of them locked in internment camps, or worse, kill them on sight.

God, he'd been here a long time.

Maybe just being locked in this place with nothing to look at but four white walls was some kind of torture. Of course the longer they waited the better. Everyone would have time to get away and regroup somewhere. Why even if they came in right now with the worst kind of torture, they could imagine, he could still hold out a little while. It would give everyone just enough time to get away, find a place to.....

No, it was nothing. Whoever it was had walked by. Ha! He had caught himself. He was frightened for a moment. He would have to prepare himself better. Not be afraid when they really came in.

They had emptied his pockets. Somehow he hadn't even noticed it when they had dragged him in here. His wallet, passport, Lana's picture all gone. In an instant they take the contents of your pockets and open up your life. What could they learn about him from his wallet? Not much. He had some money, a driver's license, his college ID card (expired). The passport would show he was a tourist. Yes, he would appear to be nothing more than an American college student on holiday. Yes, that would be how he would play it out. He was just a visitor. He didn't know anything.

His cousin David had been caught by the police in the U.S. He didn't even see the inside of a jail cell. Lawyers. Family money and a legal defense fund supported by American supporters of the I.R.A. A very different justice system. David would be out drinking in the bars while he was here in Ireland wondering when some ape was going to come and beat him to death.

He wished he could relax enough to sleep or something. He imagined all the people who were sleeping in houses, outside, even in the soldier's quarters. Perhaps everyone there at the club was home asleep in bed now.

If he couldn't sleep, maybe he should pray. Father Kilclooney would tell him to pray if he were here.

"Our father who art in ... why the Hell don't they come in and get it over with!"

Maybe they thought this would soften him up. Making him sit in here thinking like this. Well they were wrong. He would think about other things... Hugh's sister Lana. He remembered looking up from that breakfast she'd made for him. Her eyes were such a soft pale blue. And she had blushed! He could hardly remember seeing an American girl blush.

Her hair wasn't a bright red like Hugh's. It wasn't wiry like a lot of redheads. Yes, her hair was softer, a strawberry blond kind of red. He felt his skin warming as he thought about her...

The door! Christ. Michael swallowed hard. Three uniformed men entered the room and set up a folding table and a chair. They moved back and stood in the semi-darkness while a fourth man entered the room.

Michael watched as he placed a note pad and file folder on the table and seated himself.

The man's face was round, almost cherub-like. He had a single tuff of blondish hair toward the front and center of his head. The rest of his skull was covered in pinkish skin. His eyes were small. His baby-like hands opened the file folder and he stared at it. Michael noticed that he moved his entire head and neck as he read rather than moving just his eyes. Pinkface turned a page and Michael stood watching.

"Why have I been taken here?" asked Michael.

Pinkface didn't even look up. His baby hand took off from the desk like a small bird and leveled palm out toward him to indicate silence was required.

Michael sat watching. He waited until Pinkface had turned the last page, and finally looked up.

"Michael Patrick O'Shea?" the Pinkface said in a voice so nasal Michael nearly burst out laughing.

"You are Michael Patrick O'Shea?"

"Yes." replied Michael.

"We know who you are. We just wanted to see if you would admit your identity freely."

"I have no reason to deny it. I've done nothing wrong."

Pinkface looked directly at Michael without blinking his tiny eyes. "You are a member and supporter of an organization called "Noraid". "Is that correct."

"No."

"It is an organization in the United States that funnels money directly to the terrorist organization known as the Irish Republican Army and you are a member of Noraid. Is that correct?"

"No, wrong on both counts."

"Mr. O'Shea. It does you absolutely no good to lie. We have a complete file on you. We know your cousin, David Murphy, was involved in shipping arms to the I.R.A. and that you have replaced him while he is under indictment in the United States."

I have a cousin named David Murphy but I don't know anything at all about the rest."

Pinkface smiled and that unnerved Michael. His teeth were tiny and barely extended beyond the gumline.

"Michael Patrick O'Shea. I am a very patient man. You are hardly the first or last person I have talked with in this room. Your lies will not help your cause. You only convince me that I have a great deal to learn from you." Pinkface clicked his pen and began writing notes on his pad. The illegible handwriting was impossible for Michael to decode from his standing position opposite him.

"Mr. O'Shea, you entered the Republic of Ireland smuggling arms. Arms, that you and IRA operative, Hugh Doherty, smuggled here to Belfast. Is that not correct?"

Michael sat still. They know Hugh's name. What else did they know? How long had they been on to him?

"I am an American citizen. I wish to speak to someone in the United States embassy." Michael replied.

Pinkface looked at him. "Answer my question, Mr. O'Shea. "Why? What's the point? You'll just call me a liar. I want to speak directly to someone in the American Embassy."

"Mr. O'Shea, you are connected to a terrorist organization. Your government has condemned terrorism. Do you really think they will help you? We have been engaged in major seizures of illegal weapons. October 17, 1971, we captured arms at Schipol Airport in Amsterdam. March 28, 1973 we captured a 298 ton vessel off the Irish coast; it was loaded with automatic rifles, explosives and anti-tank mines. On the Fourth of July, 1975, we intercepted a variety of weapons being shipped out of Canada, 166 crates of weapons including bazooka and rocket launchers, and Kalashnikov rifles."

"We are well aware of what your organization has been up to Mr. O'Shea. Do you honestly think that your government or any civilized government on earth would support the blood bath your arms shipments have caused in Ulster?"

Michael was tempted to reply. He wanted so much to argue and justify. He wanted to shout that the British forces were an army of occupation. Arms were needed to resist them. He held off. He calmed himself and spoke softly to Pinkface.

"Why are you telling me all this? I'm just a recent college graduate here on holiday. I'm not connected to anything you've just described. I'd like to speak to someone from the American embassy."

"Mr. O'Shea. I am a patient man. Let me assure you that the direst consequences will result if you continue to refuse to cooperate with me. If I should prove unsuccessful, I will be replaced here and they will...put pressure on you."

Michael thought for a moment. This man was threatening him with torture. "What do you want?" Michael asked.

Pinkface smiled. "You were at a club in attendance of a gathering of international terrorists. We want to know the names of the leaders who were there. We want to know who is connected to your arms smuggling organization. Tell me the names of the leaders."

"Names?" asked Michael.

"Yes, names." replied Pinkface.

Michael looked at the tiny--eyed man.

"Hugh Cary, Mario Biaggi..."

The Pinkface started writing quickly, "Paul O'Dwyer, Terrence "Tip" O'Neill...Daniel Patrick Moynihan..."

"Wait!" The Pinkface shouted.

"Senator Edward Kennedy..."

The Pinkface pounded on the little table. "These are the names of American politicians!"

"You asked me for names. I'm American. Those are our leaders."

"Enough, Mr. O'Shea. I'm sorry but I will have to turn you over to my colleagues." Pinkface stood up, picked up his notepad and left taking the three men who had stood in the darkness with him.

They took the chair and table. The door closed and Michael thought to himself that it appeared he had won. He smiled to himself. Then they turned off the light and left him in the darkness.

Dubh

The lack of light makes passage of time difficult to measure. Michael on occasion heard people walking by. He felt hungry but not painfully hungry, so he couldn't have been here more than a few hours. He found a place to stretch out and lay down on the cement floor. It was cold so he hugged his arms about his chest and put his fingers into his armpits. He let his mind go back to the first night with Lana and the smell of her peat fire. He felt himself drifting off to sleep.

He awoke to pounding on the door. It sounded like ten men all pounding their fists on the door. They were screaming obscenities at him.

After a few minutes, it subsided and Michael tried to sleep again. No sooner had he started to doze and then they started pounding and shouting again. The pounding on the door started again. Michael moved his hands to cover his ears. They were shouting about what they would do to him when they came in, and what parts of his body they would cut off. Michael pressed the palms of his hands tighter over his ears.

Michael thought about Lana. He saw her face in detail. Lingering in it now, he could see in his mind, the texture of her lips and the feel of her skin, even the flutter of her eyelids all in a sensuous slow motion. The shouting at the door and pounding began to fade away and Michael fell asleep with Lana's arms around him. She became the world and Michael escaped into her.

He awoke to a nudge and opened his eyes to see Pinkface staring down at him.

"I trust you slept well Mr. O'Shea?" Michael nodded.

"Good. I want you to know that I have persuaded my superiors to give me one more chance to convince you to give me the names I've asked for. Quite frankly they can't wait to get at you. They regularly beat confessions from prisoners like yourself every day. I dare say half the confessions aren't even true. Their techniques are so effective prisoners find themselves confessing to things they didn't do..." He paused and looked into Michael's eyes. "You really would be much better off if you talked to me. Right now, you're whole. All those fingers and toes are in place and unbroken. All you've lost is a bit of sleep. Look at who you are protecting? Don't you think they would give us your name if they were here instead of you?"

Michael stared back. "I don't know any names. I am an American tourist and I want to speak with someone in the American embassy."

Pinkface stuck out his lower lip in mock sympathy. Michael could smell bacon on his breath. He was feeling hungry. "Its all right. I supported wild causes in my youth, too. I was once a member of the socialist party. Really. No one will hold this against you years from now. Foolish youth. Just tell me the names of the men you met at the club and we'll send you back to your loving parents in America. I know it may be hard to believe, but in this place, I am your friend. I understand what it is like when you give yourself to a cause." Michael swallowed. "I was at a club in Belfast. I had some drinks but I didn't know anyone there. I'm only an American tourist. I don't know anything about the I.R.A. I can't tell you anything."

Pinkface went red with anger. He moved within an inch of Michael's nose and shouted, "Damn you! Liar!" Pinkface picked up his notebook and the three men in the darkness automatically seemed to recognize this as a signal to pick up his chair and folding table. The door opened and they left.

Michael glanced up at the single light bulb expecting darkness again. No. This time the light stayed on. Michael had no idea how much time had passed. Less than 24 hours he guessed. His lips were dry and he felt some slight hunger. There was no toilet in the room. Without food or water he hadn't felt the need to go yet. In the U.S., they'd have to release him or charge him with something after 24 hours. This was British territory. No Bill of Rights. They could hold him as long as they wanted.

The door suddenly burst open. Two guards shoved a man into the room. His hands bound behind him, barefoot and limping. They pushed him onto the floor next to Michael. The man's face came into view. His eyes were both swollen shut and his front teeth were missing. The man's hair was dirty and matted, and clotted with bits of dried blood. The fingers on his left hand had been twisted backward and broken. Michael recognized him only by the underlying red color of his hair. "Hugh?"

The man on the floor moaned and nodded weakly. "Hugh?" Michael said again. The figure on the floor hissed through broken teeth. "The room is bugged." he mumbled.

Hugh spit a jelly-like blob of blood on the floor. "Don't talk to them Michael. Say nothing. If you tell them anything they'll think you know more...and they'll try to beat it out of you. Trust me. I know."

"Michael, I can't see...can open my eyes a slit. They beat my sides. Think my kidneys are bruised. I know I pissed red yesterday."

Michael sat Hugh up in the corner and peeled the duct tape off his wrists. Hugh blew a relaxed breath out through puckered lips.

"Oh, Michael," he moaned, " can the Irish throw a party or what?"

Michael smiled ."I don't know if this is a good time to tell you or not...I'm in love with your sister. Is it okay if I steal her away?"

Hugh's lips parted into a grimace that was close to a smile. Michael could see the two broken bloody front teeth. "Get her far from here, Michael."

The door opened again. A chair was set up and Michael was thrown into it. He started to curse at them. A sudden punch deep into his stomach drew all the air out of him. Michael felt his hands pulled back behind the chair and then heard the sound of duct tape going tightly about his wrists and ankles.

Hugh, hearing the commotion, pulled his body into a ball and covered his head with his hands.

Michael tried to throw his body out of the chair, and was shoved back violently. A hand pushed solidly into the center of his chest. Michael stared into the face of the guard who was pushing against him with all his weight. The guard's hair was cropped military short and his nose was bent to the left. His teeth were yellow and his breath was stale.

"Did he tell you he signed a confession?" the bent-nose said. "Did he tell you he named you as an arms supplier to a terrorist group?"

Hugh called back from the floor. "I didn't. He's lying!" Bent-nose released Michael and kicked Hugh in the ribs. Hugh wheezed out a long miserable groan... Then, he shuddered in pain.

The Bent-nose turned back to Michael. He moved so close Michael could see his skin pores and the little hairs sticking out of his nose. "Why don't you rat him out? He signed a confession. You're named as an illegal arms smuggler. That's 20 years in prison. Don't let him get away with it. Tell us what we need to know, eh?"

Michael said nothing. He tried to move his head to pull back from the bent-nose man. The sharp British accent was like a fingernail on a chalkboard.

Bent-nose's brown eyes sparkled and he smiled slightly. "Is it cause...you shagged his sister? Is that it? You feel loyal to him cause his sister gave you a little? Let me tell you about these Irish girls. I been 'ere 5 years. They all act very Catholic and proper but you buy 'em a drink and they'll be sliding your pole like any whore."

Michael tried to move his head the other way. Bent-nose's stinking breath was making him sick

"Personally, I don't like the Teigh pussy. The Irish bitches are too hairy. Hair on their lips and even their nipples. American girls shave everything, don't they? Now, if I was you...If I thought that pathetic pile of Fenian shit over there on the floor had sold me out for 20 years...I'd talk. I'd do whatever it took to get me back to America and all those clean-shaven American cheerleader women."

"Those Irish girls are all crawling with crotch crickets anyway."

Michael had all he could stand. He gritted his teeth together and glared at the bent-nosed man.

"Shut up!" He screamed.

Bent-nose laughed. "Oh, ho-ho-ho! I touched a nerve, didn't I?" He suddenly lashed out and Michael felt an explosion of fire on his cheek, over and over again as Bent-nose repeatedly slapped him.

His ears rang and tears ran down his face. Michael could feel mucus running from his nose onto his upper lip. He sobbed.

"Oh, look." said Bent-nose. "I've hurt you. You're sniveling. What are you going to do when I really hurt you, eh? What will you do when I cut things off?"

Michael held his breath. He could hear his heart pounding in his ears. His stomach was aching from being hit and his cheeks were burning from the slaps. He closed his eyes...he waited. He thought of Lana. He could see her face in his mind. Her pale blue eyes were filled with tears. She wept with him and slowly Michael became aware of the silence in the room. He opened his eyes and everyone was gone. The only trace of them was the small spot of blood Hugh had left on the cement floor.

Michael took a deep breath and suddenly felt his bladder release. God. He'd wet himself. Now his humiliation was complete. He could at least console himself knowing he hadn't been broken. He had told them nothing. His hands had gone numb and his arms ached from being pulled back behind the chair.

He could hear talking outside the door. Nothing they said was clear. He could hear Bent-nose and Pink-face. They were arguing. Maybe now they'd play the "good cop-bad cop routine" with him. He'd had psychological torture and a bit of physical abuse. Now what would they do to him?

The door! Christ! He swallowed hard and tried to maintain some form of a brave front. The door opened wide. A soldier in a khaki uniform entered. A black hood was pulled over Michael's head. His hands remained taped together but he was freed from the chair. He was pulled to his feet. It was hard to breathe, the hood was sucked into his mouth and nose.

"Walk." Strong hands gripped his arms and guided him. "To the left!" Michael obeyed.

"To the right now!" He turned again. The tile floor made a clicking sound with every footstep. He could hear the soldier's steps were only a little behind his own. Suddenly, he felt the hood yanked up and off his head. He was at the end of a hall. A guard stood in front of a door.

The guard swung out an arm and the door opened to the fresh air. Rain was pouring down over the barbed-wired grounds of the barracks. Eyeing a pistol at his center, he halted at the doorway as the nuzzle came close to his stomach. The gun waved him on and Michael stepped out into the downpour. A knife split the tape holding his hands. They pushed his jacket on him and shoved his wallet and passport into his pocket.

"Get out!"

"What?"

"You heard me. Go back to your flat or wherever the hell you're staying."

Michael looked back at the form. He could see the gun but not the man's face. The soldier's entire body was in darkness. Rain was soaking into Michael's jacket. He pulled it around himself, still looking with disbelief at the figure in the doorway. What was he saying? Did this mean he was free to go?

"Well, go on! We've no more use for you!"

"What?" Anger, outrage, replaced fear. "You think you can just pull someone off the street, throw him in a room, beat him and then let him go with no explanation!"

"We can. In this country, we can."

The rain was running down Michael's face, his hair matted. Michael's face tightened and suddenly he felt his grandfather's voice roar out of him. "The people of Ireland are fed up with your kind! They've rebelled against you before and they will again! If it takes me the rest of my life, I'll make sure Ireland is free of you!"

"Listen, Yank! Your kind of rabble-rousing led to all this! Stay out of it! We don't need you stirring things up more! Go kiss the Blarney Stone, buy yourself a walking stick, and get the hell back to your own fucking country!"

"This is my country." Michael turned away and walked through the gates.

Another soldier came out of the barracks and lit a cigarette. "Is that the one?" he asked, watching Michael walk into the streetlights in the drizzling rain.

"Yeah, that's him." said the other.

A stream of rainwater ran off the roof and put out his cigarette. He broke it and snapped it away into the gutter. He looked back up and saw Michael's silhouetted form far off down the road.

"I hope someone said a prayer for that poor bastard."

Michael walked down toward Donegal Street. His clothes were soaked and his feet were cold and wet. The rain had washed away the dried tears and mucus from his face. His pants were totally wet now and hid the tell-tale urine stain. His eyes and cheeks still burned. He could feel himself shake as he walked. He was in a kind of shock he told himself. He splashed some water from a puddle over his face. He needed to think a bit. He would stay on the back streets. They might be dark and have poor drainage but the main roads would have soldiers guarding them. He would work his way back to Duddy's flat. The rain was coming harder now. The streetlights shining from the next block over created strange shadows on the buildings. The ruins of an old movie house had a twisted look to them. The burned and broken walls seemed almost ablaze with light reflecting from the rain-coated surface.

The sound of running feet came from the alley just ahead. Michael moved back into the shadows. The running stopped. A blond-haired man came into the light. Michael recognized him as one of the battalion commanders at the club.

"O'Brien" Michael said aloud. A pistol swung towards his face. Three other men entered the light. Michael remembered two of them. One was Gilmore and the other McDuid. The last one, a bald man was a complete stranger. Their faces were blank, their eyes staring. They moved closer. He could see wounds now. McDuid was holding a bleeding arm. O'Brien had a cut above his eye. A strand of blond hair soaked with blood hung down in the wound. The pistol in O'Brien's hand remained centered at Michael.

"What's happened?" Michael asked.

"The British Army has swept into the no-go areas. They've come in and rounded up everyone they can. They're interning every one in the area into camps."

"They took Hugh and I outside the club."

McDuid started at Michael. "How'd you escape?" he asked.

"I didn't. They just let me go." replied Michael.

"Let you go? They never just let you go. They never just let anyone go. What did you tell them?"

"Nothing."

"Where is Hugh Dorherty then?" demanded McDuid.

"I don't know. They beat him up and broke his fingers. I don't even know if he is still alive."

"Seven men lost their lives tonight. I don't know how many interned and I think this Yank sold us out!"

"What?"

"I didn't inform."

"You're a bloody tout! Why'd they let you go?"

"No. The Brits must have let me go to make it look like I informed!"

O'Brien looked toward each of the other men and placed his pistol in his belt. Michael stood frozen as the four men encircled him. Suddenly one sent a fist into his stomach. He collapsed, a second blow struck him in the kidney. More punches, the back, the head, stomach, kidneys.

He was on the ground looking up, their legs standing all around him. A boot lifted and smashed down on his side. Pain exploded.

He started to get up. A single kick to the face forced him down again. More kicks to the sides. It was hard to breathe now. He was coughing. Something seemed caught in his throat. It was coming out of his mouth. He was hacking it out. Blood.

Rolling from side to side. Blood running from his nose. Another foot came down, the crotch.

He shuddered. God! Please, stop. Everything was a blur. Lana. It hit again in the side.

"Mary, Queen of Ireland..." The Face. Every breath choked. The stomach, the sides...He couldn't draw a breath.

The pain became something apart from him. He became aware of a gun shot roaring into his ears.

The kicking stopped. He closed his eyes and waited for silence. It came.

Siochan
Sinan Sceale

Michael's eyes fluttered open. He was aware of a wheezing sound and slowly realized it was his own breathing. Someone was sitting beside him. Someone was fixing his hair and dabbing at his wounds.

"Michael. You awake? Can you understand me?" It was Duddy's voice.

"I stopped them Michael. I had to shoot in the air over their heads but I stopped them. I told them the raid started while you were still in the club with us. You couldn't have informed."

Michael nodded. Drool ran from his lip onto his shirt.

"Don't blame them. Its a common Brit trick to make us turn on each other. They were insane with anger. The British just rounded up hundreds for the internment camps. They needed someone to blame. I'm truly sorry Michael. Often they just don't see the big picture. We have agents on the inside, inside the barracks. We forwarded the records of your capture to the U.S. Embassy. What they did to you will be on the news in the U.S. tonight."

Michael's eyes opened. He was surprised.

"You can follow what I'm saying Michael?" Michael nodded again.

"Good. It is important to me that you understand. You see, Michael, the I.R.A. has many enemies: The Ulster Defense Force, the British Army, and the entire British Establishment. Ignorance is our enemy. We even have enemies through default. When we knock the gate off someone's garden while moving against the British troops we send someone round to repair the gate. We don't want to turn a neutral into an enemy because we inconvenienced someone. We need support. Help. You know why the Brits ended the death penalty for the I.R.A.? A dead I.R.A. soldier became a martyr, a hero. We'd write songs about them, so now they intern us and bleed the life out of our young men and women one day at a time."

"I don't believe we can be defeated but I don't want this bloody war to go on forever either. I've lost my son and most of my adult life to this struggle. I've seen far too many widows and children weeping beside coffins. It has to end Michael. You came here to Northern Ireland to help bring this war to an end didn't you?"

Michael nodded weakly.

"You're a student of history... Duddy continued. "Do you know why the British didn't kill Eamon DeValera along with the other Irish rebels back in 1916? It's because he was like you. He was an Irish-American. Born in New York State. He even had a Spanish surname, very American. The British were at war with Germany. They couldn't afford to antagonize their American allies. Eamon DeValera lived to become the President of the Irish Republic. The same Irish Republic that left six counties of Ireland in British hands. The very six counties we're still fighting for more than 50 years later."

"Michael, can you imagine what might have happened if the Brits had killed DeValera? Think of how angry the Irish-Americans would have been if the Brits had pushed one of their citizens against a wall, without a trial and shot him? If they had just executed an American citizen like they executed one of us?"

"America is even more powerful today. A superpower. Britain has become comparatively weak. What do you think America would do today if the word got out that the British had captured a young American tourist, imprisoned him, tortured him, beat him, ...and later killed him?"

"We could play up the fact that the British were the same people that the Americans fought in their Revolution. Who was it that burned the White House in the War of 1812 and later sided with the South in the American Civil War? The Brits! What would be said if those bloody British bastards killed a young American tourist! The Americans would be outraged.

"I believe that the 40 million Americans of Irish ancestry would never stand for it, and we wouldn't have to go on and on with our bloody armed struggle for years and years. The Brits would be forced to talk peace. It would be a way to end this war. It would save lives."

'Do you understand, Michael?"

Michael nodded his head, the full weight of Duddy's words reaching into him.

"We need an American martyr for our cause. We need an Irish-American hero."

Duddy drew a British officer's pistol. Placed the muzzle against Michael's left ear and fired.

THE END

About the Author

Dan Sheehan grew up Irish American in Syracuse, New York and graduated from Syracuse University. He holds a BA in Creative Writing and an MS in English Education. He has traveled extensively in Ireland and spent the last twenty years teaching English in Bethel, Kodiak and Craig, Alaska.